Using the New In Chess app is easy!

- get early access to every issue
- replay all games in the Gameviewer

1

Sign in with your username and password to access the digital issue.

2

Read the article, optimized for your screen size.

3

Click on the Gameviewer button to get to the built-in chess board.

4

Replay the game, including an option to analyze with Stockfish.

The chess magazine that moves

www.newinchess.com/chess-apps

'Chess is 100% tactics.'

TEAM **CHINA**
WEI YI / DING LIREN / WANG HAO / HOU YIFAN / YU YANGYI / JU WENJUN

White to play

CONTRIBUTORS TO THIS ISSUE
Simen Agdestein, Johan-Sebastian Christiansen, Maxim Dlugy, Anish Giri, John Henderson, Alexander Münninghoff, Maxim Notkin, Arthur van de Oudeweetering, Judit Polgar, Matthew Sadler, Han Schut, Nigel Short, Jan Timman, Thomas Willemze, Yu Yangyi, Hou Yifan

Back in business

New York park chess hustlers struck a defiant note back in April that despite a pandemic lockdown, they would still be open for business at their usual pitches. But the coronavirus reality hit hard in what became the epicentre of the US outbreak, and even those steely street-fighters were banished, having to observe several weeks of shelter-in-place restrictions.

However in early May, when the weather got warmer, and the restrictions began to ease in the bustling metropolis, they were soon back in business. And as they emerged, photographer Juan Arredondo captured this scene for The New York Times as the chess battles resumed at J. Hood Wright Park in Washington Heights. Arredondo was both surprised and uplifted to see so many playing chess again. Though the players all wore masks, and many seemed to be socially-distancing a chess table from each other, there did seem to be a lack of gloves and hand sanitizers on display for added Covid-19 protection. The photographer reported that just as he captured this image, police officers arrived to warn the kibitzers to keep a reasonable distance from each other, and those watching this game soon dispersed. ∎

Sage advice

As the British government comes under mounting criticism for its response to the coronavirus pandemic, Prime Minister Boris Johnson and his aides defend themselves with the daily media mantra that they will 'always be guided by the science'. A prominent role is played by Downing Street's secretive scientific advisory group, Sage. But who are they?

At the end of April, Google confirmed that one of its senior executives had participated in the UK government's top-level scientific advisory group and he is someone who might know a thing or two about strategy and planning. After all, he's from the chess community!

Former child chess prodigy Demis Hassabis, a co-founder of Google's artificial intelligence division, DeepMind – which revolutionized chess with its 'game changer' AI system AlphaZero – was invited to attend Sage meetings in mid-March, when the group was considering whether the UK should go into lockdown.

Google said Hassabis was invited by the chief scientific adviser, Sir Patrick Vallance, and it's thought that Hassabis, a world-leading AI researcher, was brought on board

Will Demis Hassabis create another game changer?

to offer advice and insight into AI developments for helping to find a vaccine and Covid-19 track and trace apps.

Billions

One of the great things about a lockdown is that you can at least binge-view with impunity all your TV favourites. One not-to-be-missed is Showtime's 'Billions', the gripping drama all about power and greed as US Attorney Chuck Rhoades (Paul Giamatti) goes after hedge

Hikaru Nakamura honoured Mike Birbiglia with a flashy mate.

fund kingpin Bobby 'Axe' Axelrod (Damian Lewis) in a battle between two powerful New York figures.

The fifth season of the award-winning show got underway during the lockdown period, and one of its underlying themes has become chess – with a wonderful cameo from one of the world's top grandmasters! In Episode 2, 'The Chris Rock Test', reigning US champion Hikaru Nakamura appears in the show to play himself.

It's all staged around Axe's financial retreat where a charity fundraising simultaneous display is organized after some of the central characters had been bragging about their chess-playing prowess. Beautifully filmed in an atmospheric wood-panelled room, the chess scene, with Staunton wooden chess sets, tables and digital clocks a-plenty, had Nakamura – also known for his interest in the financial markets – turning in an Emmy-winning performance, if only there was a chess master cameo category!

One of the key moments witnessed Nakamura delivering a pictur-

esque mate-in-four after sacrificing his queen against Oscar Langstraat (played by stand-up comedian Mike Birbiglia), the show's Silicon Valley token nerd.

Hikaru Nakamura
Oscar Langstraat

1.♖xg7+! ♔xg7 2.♘f5+ ♔g8 3.♖g6+!! fxg6 4.♘h6 Mate.

Birbiglia bigged up the chess episode, tweeting: 'I learned to become a Chessmaster. Like every great method actor I also "unlearned" it. It was the responsible thing to do. (An honour to meet chess champion Hikaru Nakamura.)'

A really difficult life

The chess-themed movie *Critical Thinking* was supposed to premiere during this year's SXSW – South by Southwest, the annual mid-March music and film festival in Austin, Texas – before Covid-19 upended the film industry and stopped the

Ace student Marcel (Jeffry Batista) stuns class and teacher with his blindfold play.

festival. But before the premiere, there was a special screening for reviewers, and the critics began to publish their praise of the movie ahead of its theatrical release.

Set in Miami in 1998, *Critical Thinking* is the true-life underdog, Latino-inspired story of underprivileged high school students who defied the odds with a team of mostly low-income, minority students to win a national chess tournament. The film, described by one critic as '*Dangerous Minds* meets *Searching for Bobby Fischer*', is directed by and stars John Leguizamo in the lead role of the inspiration Miami Jackson Senior High School teacher/chess coach 'Mr. T' Mario Martinez.

'I think the film really shows the horrors, neglect, abandonment and wasted talent you find in these places,' said Leguizamo in an interview. 'I wanted it to be real. I didn't want it to represent Disney. I wanted to show the obstacles these kids are running away from. They're not just "underprivileged". It's a really difficult life.'

The Lockdown Showdown

Last issue, in our Fair & Square column, Ivan Ljubicic, coach to Roger Federer, made a guest appearance. The former world number 3 encouraged tennis fans missing live action to hunker down during the lockdown to follow the FIDE Candidates Tournament, as he was.

It seems that chess-mad Ljubicic's encouragement for court-side fans to stay safe by following the action in Yekaterinburg caught the eye of Maxime Vachier-Lagrave. When MVL returned home from the 'adjourned' Candidates, he arranged to play in a 'Lockdown Showdown' Lichess simultaneous and reached out to the Croatian former tennis star to be one of the 24 players to take part.

MVL ended with 21 wins, 2 draws and one loss – and one of those draws was against Ljubicic in a no-holds

In a Najdorf labyrinth, former tennis star Ivan Ljubicic held MVL to a draw.

barred Sicilian Najdorf. There was some suspicion of backhand engine help being deployed, but MVL sportingly gave his opponent the benefit of the doubt. 'I got lucky multiple times,' tweeted Ljubicic after the simul. 'I thank MVL for giving me the opportunity to play against him and being so kind. I hope [he] wins the Candidates and I will then consider preparing him for Magnus Carlsen!'

Express yourself

According to many scientific experts, wearing a face mask could help prevent the spread of coronavirus. We see many styles when we dare to venture out of the safety of our homes and onto the streets, and now there's even a mask that's suitable for the discerning chess player.

The non-medical 'Obsessive Chess Disorder' face mask, claims its designer in the blurb on the global online marketplace for independent

Who's that girl? Ah, a chess player!

artists at Redbubble, 'helps you express yourself even when you can't show your face.' It's made of two layers of soft 100% brushed polyester, comes in one adult size of 7.25" x 4.6" / 18.5 x 11.5 cm, over-ear elastic straps for a snug fit over mouth and nose, and costs £10.14 plus postage and packing.

They come with the warning not to use them as medical personal protective equipment and the advice to wash them after each use.

Back to normal

There is a light at the end of the dark coronavirus tunnel, as one tiny chess-loving nation is showing. Iceland was the first European country to cancel a

Robert Lagerman of the ICF knows what it takes to run a post-lockdown tournament.

major chess event, the Reykjavik Open, and now they have been the first to restart again, reports federation president Gunnar Björnsson.

Iceland weathered the pandemic well with 1,803 cases of the virus, 10 deaths, and now only three left in self-isolation. Apart from early vigilance, its success is being attributed partly to its tiny population of around 364,000.

And so on Saturday 23 May, as the country began to re-open with confidence once again, sport events for children under 16 were allowed – and leading the way was chess, with 26 teams taking part in the first post-lockdown over-the-board tournament, the Icelandic School Championship U-13. ∎

Sultan Khan

It is unfortunate that the life story of my late grandfather, Sultan Khan, has been misrepresented in recent years. Daniel King's recent book, *Sultan Khan – The Indian Servant who became Chess Champion of the British Empire* (and his article based on the book in New In Chess 2020/2) adds to what was largely an online trend of sensational reporting. In this letter, I feel compelled to correct some salient misconceptions emanating from King's book.

At the outset it must be mentioned that most of the errors in King's work emerge from the simple fact that he chose not to contact any of Sultan Khan's family members or sources in Pakistan (the country of Khan's residence and death) while writing this book. Instead he has relied on secondary sources and online materials, which are unfortunately not that accurate. Here I would also acknowledge his diligence in collecting and analysing my grandfather's chess games – those sections are clearly well worth reading.

There are three main misconceptions about Sultan Khan that I wish to focus on in this piece. The book has many more but correcting them all would require a complete re-write of the sections pertaining to biography.

First is the question of his nationality. King declares Khan to be an 'Indian servant' on the book cover and at several places throughout the narrative. This is problematic for several reasons. Formally speaking, Sultan Khan was a British subject for the first 44 years of his life (1903-47) and then a very proud Pakistani citizen from 1947 till his demise in 1966. He had no connection with the country that is now India other than for transit during travel or to play tournament matches, something that he also did in England, Czech Republic, Switzerland, etc. That does not make him a citizen of these countries any more than it makes him an Indian. Moreover, given the tense

political realities of the region, King should have been careful and sensitive before proclaiming him as such, as he has denied a dead man his conscious decision of statehood. Khan *chose* to be resident in Pakistan and contrary to King's assertion that he offered no political opinions, Khan was a patriot and believed firmly in Pakistan, a homeland created for South Asia's Muslim population in 1947.

Muslim citizens of the sub-continent, led by Muhammad Ali Jinnah, fought hard to have an independent state of Pakistan and to deny their nationhood, as King has done for Khan, is akin to denying one of the

also a denial of Khan's political inclinations and actions.

Secondly, King has cast Sultan Khan as a 'servant' who was dependent on the feudal Malik Umar Tiwana's largesse to survive. This is based on various online and western accounts and is untrue. Sultan Khan belonged to the Awan tribe of the Punjab and hailed from a respected family of *pirs* (religious saints who are based at a shrine and have a devoted following) and landowners that traced their lineage to Mughal times. Khan's family, locally known as the Mianas, were not only the religious leaders of their area but also the *numberdaars*

Sultan Khan's stay at Umar Tiwana's estate was not in a servile capacity, but because Tiwana requested him to form a chess team.

biggest movements of self-determination of the twentieth century. Khan was born in Mitha Tiwana in the Khushab district of the Punjab, present-day Pakistan, and spent the entirety of his life (save domestic and international travel to play chess matches) in the same area. So classifying him as an 'Indian' is not only factually wrong but

and *zaildaars* (titles awarded to leading landlords of an area by the British). The Tiwanas themselves, on the other hand, derived their entire fortune from British patronage as can be verified by colonial records as well as all major political histories of colonial Punjab. Sultan Khan's stay at Umar Tiwana's estate was therefore

The participants in Berne 1932. In front row, between Euwe and Bogoljubow, Sultan Khan stands reading.

not in a servile capacity, but because Tiwana requested him in 1926 to form a chess team there that he would then promote at home and abroad. Tiwana promised Khan a monthly stipend and board and lodging in return. Their relationship was one of mutual respect for Tiwana's family also recognised Sultan's family as their *pirs* or religious guides, and had done so for generations. Indeed the religious shrine in question, known as Mian Athar Sahib's darbar, is extant and active to this day, passed on through primogeniture to various heirs of Khan's father. (As a younger son, he did not inherit the status of *pir* himself.) Interestingly, R.N. Coles' biography of Khan also mentions that Khan's father was a 'religious leader' but fails to grasp the social and political influence such a role carried.

The assertion that Tiwana gifted a farmstead to Khan for subsistence is also untrue as the land had been in Khan's family for generations. The property records for the same exist to this day and are easily verifiable. In fact, altogether Khan inherited 114 acres of land from his father in two separate locations and that is where he derived his livelihood from. Interestingly, even western accounts of Khan in 1929, the year of his first visit to England when he won the British Chess Championship at Ramsgate, describe him as a landlord and as a 'gentleman of good family' (*Chess Amateur*, Sept. 1929, p. 265). There was a group photo taken at Ramsgate in my grandfather's private papers, now in possession of my father, which also describes him as 'a landowner in the Punjab'. It is only in later years that western commentators, perhaps owing to racism and perhaps envious of Khan's success, sought to belittle him and reduce his status, and thereby sensationalised his achievements.

Finally, Sultan Khan was not menial or lowly as King makes him out to be. It can be tempting for a certain class of writers to cast achievements of people of colour as

Write to us
New In Chess, P.O. Box 1093
1810 KB Alkmaar, The Netherlands
or e-mail: editors@newinchess.com
Letters may be edited or abridged

extraordinary and miraculous and so they seek to dehumanize them as illiterate savages defying gravity, because the truth that they could beat white men purely on merit is too hard to bear. As a scholar of empire, I am only too familiar with such trends, neatly summed up by the Palestinian scholar Edward Said in his seminal work *Orientalism* (1978). Khan was far from illiterate or uncivilised and we possess his notes and diaries to this day. He spoke conversational English, read both Arabic and Urdu and was certainly not without thoughts and opinions, political or otherwise. In a photograph from Berne taken in 1932, he can also be seen intently reading some material.

These are just a few of the more salient misconceptions in King's book that I have identified. Unfortunately, it contains many more inaccuracies, from the year of Sultan's birth to the cause of his death. Frankly, it is unbelievable that such a historically inaccurate work has been published and, in all fairness, the author and publisher both owe Sultan's family an apology as well as an immediate recall/revision of this book.

Dr Atiyab Sultan
St. Louis, MO, USA

(The letter writer provided the following biographical information: Atiyab Sultan is the granddaughter of Sultan Khan. She holds MPhil and PhD degrees from the University of Cambridge, UK, where she trained as an economist and economic historian. Professionally, she is an officer of the Pakistan Administrative Service, Government of Pakistan. In writing this letter, she acknowledges the assistance of her father, Ather Sultan, Sultan Khan's eldest son, a graduate of the London School of Economics.)

Postscript Daniel King

Thank you to Dr Sultan for her critique of the book. I acknowledge the sensitivities of the issues to the family and I welcome new information and insights into Sultan Khan's life.

My research chiefly focused on Sultan Khan's time in Europe in the years 1929-1933 and that period comprises the vast majority of the book. I am glad that Dr Sultan recognises my diligence in collecting and analysing Khan's games. More than that, by researching newspapers, magazines and journals of the time, I managed to uncover stories of Sultan Khan that, I believe, provide an insight into his character and his chess style, set within the political context of the age.

Nowhere in the book have I asserted that Sultan Khan was a citizen of the modern-day state of India. He won the All-India Championship in 1928 and in newspapers and journals of the 1920s and 1930s Khan was described as Indian. I should emphasise that none of this denies his Pakistani citizenship from 1947.

Regarding Sultan Khan's status, I included in the book that the family owned land and that Khan's father was a religious leader. I was unaware of the extent of the family landholdings and the details of the family's heritage, and naturally that provides a much richer picture of Sultan Khan's background.

The description 'servant' from the strap line refers to the relationship between Sir Umar Hayat Khan and Sultan Khan. Sir Umar Hayat Khan was honorary Aide-de-Camp to King George V, as well as a senior advisor to the British government, and a member of the Indian upper house. Sultan Khan was an employee in his household.

I was influenced by the phrasing of reports which stated, for example, that Sultan Khan 'was brought to England by Sir Umar Hayat Khan' (*The Times* 10 August 1929); and 'when he went to England he took Sultan with him'

(*The Game of Chess – Western and Native Methods* by Tamannacharya Padsalgikar 1941). Or this from an English newspaper report: 'At his house in Kensington Sir Umar keeps almost feudal state, Sultan Khan, who won the British championship at his first attempt, is the Prince's court chess player' (*Northern Daily Mail* 16 August 1932). Reuben Fine writes of visiting Sir Umar Hayat Khan's house in 1933 with the rest of the American chess team where, '... we found ourselves in the peculiar position of being waited on at table' by Sultan Khan.

The trope that Sultan Khan was illiterate has been repeated in articles on many occasions and was one that I was keen to debunk. In a newspaper report after his first British Championship success, it is stated that he had spent much of his youth studying the Koran and 'he has earned the title "Hafiz!", accorded to one who is able to repeat from memory the whole of the Koran' (*Manchester Guardian* 13 August 1929). This was included in the book.

Harry Golombek, one of the English players at the time, writes about his first meeting with Sultan Khan and describes him as 'totally uneducated' – to which I took exception in the book.

Sultan Khan's early interviews in England were conducted through an interpreter, but, with time, his English improved. During the latter period of his stay in London it is evident that Khan's spoken English was proficient and I am glad to say that I found direct quotes from him, which I included in the book.

All the sources I consulted (newspapers, magazines, ship passenger records) indicated that Khan's year of birth was 1905. But, of course, family records take precedence.

I wrote the book as a tribute to a great player and a fine man. From the numerous primary sources that I consulted, I attempted to put forward as accurate a portrayal

of Sultan Khan as possible. I am fascinated to learn that Dr Sultan possesses notebooks and diaries belonging to Sultan Khan and it would be wonderful if they could be used to support further research into his life.

Little 'trouvailles'

First of all I want to congratulate you for your excellent magazine. Every time it drops into my mailbox it promises joyful hours of reading about the sparkling world of chess.

While I was browsing through New In Chess 2020/3, I suddenly discovered that in the games Najer-Nepomniachtchi (p. 57)

Najer-Nepomniachtchi
position after 31.♖e1

(31...g4! to follow up with 32...♕f1+! would have done the trick, but Black played 31...♕b5 and later lost the game.')
and Gosling-Rudd (p. 89)

Gosling-Rudd
position after 1...♘f4!!

(2.♗d8?? ♕f1+)

we see exactly the same mating pattern at work: a queen sacrifice on f1, followed either by a rook's mate on h1 or a knight's mate on e2! Absolutely astonishing! Fun fact: while the weaker player Rudd spotted it, ten years later Nepomniachtchi didn't see it and later even lost the game.

Now I am curious to know if these two examples have been deliberately chosen to the secret amusement of the editorial staff, or if they have made their way into the magazine by chance?

Be that as it may – it is exactly for those little 'trouvailles' that I love the game and your magazine!

Stephan Arounopoulos (CC-IM)
Gerlingen, Germany

Editorial postscript

Pure coincidence! But you are not the only one who will not easily forget this neat combination! ■

COLOPHON

PUBLISHER: Allard Hoogland
EDITOR-IN-CHIEF:
Dirk Jan ten Geuzendam
HONORARY EDITOR: Jan Timman
CONTRIBUTING EDITOR: Anish Giri
EDITORS: Peter Boel, René Olthof
PRODUCTION: Joop de Groot
TRANSLATORS: Peter Boel, Piet Verhagen
SALES AND ADVERTISING: Remmelt Otten

PHOTOS AND ILLUSTRATIONS IN THIS ISSUE:
Juan Arredondo, Bas Beekhuizen, Henrik Carlsen,
Maria Emelianova, Joris van Velzen, Berend Vonk

COVER DESIGN: Helene Bergmans

© No part of this magazine may be reproduced,
stored in a retrieval system or transmitted in any
form or by any means, recording or otherwise,
without the prior permission of the publisher.

NEW IN CHESS
P.O. BOX 1093
1810 KB ALKMAAR
THE NETHERLANDS

PHONE: 00-31-(0)72-51 27 137
SUBSCRIPTIONS: nic@newinchess.com
EDITORS: editors@newinchess.com
ADVERTISING: otten@newinchess.com

WWW.NEWINCHESS.COM

'You want to watch together with friends. Be together and cheer together when a goal is scored. Otherwise we might as well watch chess.' *(A German football fan's lament as the Bundesliga resumed without spectators in the stadiums)*

Shaun Ryder: 'Our Pearl's going to teach me how to play chess. I could be a chess master.' *(During lockdown, the Happy Mondays lead singer and hell-raiser reveals to the tabloids that he's taking chess lessons from his 11-year-old daughter)*

Mikhail Botvinnik: 'The Scots revere the memory of Burns, and I was presented with a book of his verse in Glasgow. The Scots were surprised to learn that I had read Burns – they had not heard of the translation done by Marshak. "This is remarkable," said Wood, joining our conversation, "all that remains is to translate Marshak and the English will be able to read Burns."' *(In his autobiography Achieving the Aim, recalling a simultaneous tour of England and Scotland in 1967 organized by Baruch Wood, the legendary founding editor and publisher of Chess magazine)*

Chris Wakelin: 'Both chess and snooker require you to think clearly and not let your emotions get the better of you. They provide no room for rash or poor decisions.' *(Tweeted by the world number 49*

in snooker, who used his pandemic lockdown time to renew his passion for chess)

Darnay Holmes: 'I'm the type of player that wants to get insight into everything that's going on, so I walked up to the chess master and asked him "Do you mind helping me out playing chess?"' *(The late April 2020 NFL Draft pick for the New York Giants, interviewed by the New York Post, explaining how his interest in chess was piqued when he noticed several NFL stars playing the game)*

Johann Löwenthal: 'The judicious violation of general principles marks the master-mind.'

David J. Morgan: 'A chess optimist is someone who thinks he will never do anything as stupid again.' *(In his 'Quotes & Queries' column for British Chess Magazine in the late 1950s)*

Juan José Arreola: 'Poetry and chess are impossible for man, they are beyond his reach.' *(The Mexican writer and humorist, who was a lifelong chess fan, interviewed in the October 1997 edition of Ajedrez de Mexico)*

Stuart Rachels: 'Great chess games are breathtaking works of art.' *(The former chess prodigy and 1989/90 co-US Champion, and now Associate Professor of Philosophy at the University of Alabama)*

Wesley So: 'I used to study old games, but I then realized they're getting older and the computers are getting stronger.' *(Said during the 2018 Berlin Candidates)*

Alireza Firouzja: 'It depends on the day, but the only thing I think about is chess, of course – it's not anything else. Maybe the whole day.' *(Interviewed after winning through to the Chess24 Banter Blitz Cup Final)*

William Winter: 'I strongly recommend a short term of imprisonment to all those who wish to do some serious study.' *(Imprisoned in the 1920s for sedition, he used his study time well by going on to become British champion twice in the 1930s)*

Alexander Grischuk: 'I think results matter – names are just consolations.' *(Said by the Muscovite on having openings named after you, during one of his Magnus Carlsen Invitational commentary stints)*

Andrew Waterman: 'Chess resembles writing, painting and music in being an obsessional mental activity preoccupied with exploring tension and complication to resolve them to triumphant harmony.' *(The English poet was a keen chess amateur, and this was the introduction to his anthology The Poetry of Chess, where the chessboard was the subject for poets from Chaucer to the 1980s)*

Magnus Carlsen keeps winning, as he expands his business conglomerate

Working from

Magnus Carlsen looks relaxed as he is getting ready for another round of the Magnus Carlsen Invitational at his home in Oslo. The photo was taken by his father Henrik. During the games no one was allowed into the room

As borders closed and countries went in lockdown, Magnus Carlsen took the initiative and invited a select group of top players to an online super-tournament, the Magnus Carlsen Invitational. Only weeks later he started the $1M Magnus Tour. **DIRK JAN TEN GEUZENDAM** looks at the online chess boom and the World Champion's prominent role in it.

home

A nd suddenly chess found itself in the mainstream news again – almost in the way it had enjoyed such warm and prolonged attention spans when Deep Blue defeated Garry Kasparov (and mankind!), or when AI-driven program AlphaZero mastered the game in seven hours (and then beat everyone and everything).

AlphaZero seemed to show that this board game with wooden pieces was antiquated and only deserved a niche existence in these futuristic times. Now things are different. 'Chess is the New King of the Pandemic' was the headline in *The Wall Street Journal* of an article that sketched how perfectly in line with these new extraordinary times chess was. While other sports were wracking their brains about how to survive in a society of social distancing, 'grandmasters and pawn-pushers alike' are happily filling their time with 'one of the world's oldest games'. Online, at a happy distance and doing great!

The New York Times couldn't agree more and struck a similar chord. Their headline was 'Chess Thrives Online despite Pandemic', and the paper noted: 'While the outbreak has forced most sports around the world to shut down, chess has not only found a way to carry on – it is thriving in some ways. In the past several weeks, there has been a surge in grass-roots participation in chess to go along with a few high-profile professional events online.'

While they all extolled the virtues of online chess and its popularity, they didn't forget to focus on the man whose actions on and off the board created the boom. Magnus Carlsen is not only a very successful World Champion, he is also a prominent and pivotal player in the chess business. After all, it was the 29-year-old Norwegian who took the first step to keep international top-level chess going by organizing the online Magnus Carlsen Invitational and making sure there was a fat $ 250,000 prize-fund.

The Guardian wrote: 'Carlsen has been the Federer, Djokovic

'Magnus' is by far the strongest brand in chess; none of his colleagues even come close

and Nadal of chess since becoming world No 1 in 2010. Even now he is the game's great white shark, with an unnerving ability to detect weaknesses.' But probably the most fortunate and flattering comparison was made by *CNN*, which drew parallels between Carlsen and Michael Jordan, whose greatness is so vividly brought back to everyone's mind thanks to Netflix's wildly popular docuseries *The Last Dance*. In an interview with Aimee Lewis, Carlsen – who is a big basketball fan and enjoyed the series immensely – was almost relieved to agree that he understands Jordan's darker sides when he said: 'Some people in Norway have been saying: "You don't have to be an a**hole to win". Whenever they say that, from now on I'll say "go and watch Jordan" and I'm going to use it as an excuse for any questionable behaviour.'

He also happily agreed that for him, too, everything is aimed at avoiding what is worst of all: losing. 'There are no excuses. You always have to be the best; nothing else is acceptable.'

50 million US dollars

As we have seen the past years, Magnus Carlsen wants to be a leader, not only with his results but also with regard to shaping the future of his sport. 'Magnus' is by far the strongest brand in chess; none of his colleagues even come close. In addition to the pool of sponsors he already had, he signed a two-year, 200,000 euro per annum sponsorship deal with Unibet last January to become an ambassador of the betting company, which is part of the Malta-based Kindred Group. The deal was the next step in a clear dispute between Carlsen and the Norwegian Chess Federation, which voted against a three-year, 5.5 million euro sponsorship deal with Unibet last year.

With this money, Carlsen felt, the development of new talents could have been taken to a new level, but this idea clashed with social sentiment in Norway, where gambling is

a state monopoly. Unibet is hoping to end that monopoly by active lobbying, but it's a sensitive issue. All sports in Norway are supported by the profits of Norsk Tipping, and trying to end its monopoly goes against the ingrained feelings of many Norwegians.

In reaction to the failed deal, in June 2019, Carlsen created his own club Offerspill, which got support from Unibet, and he severed his ties with the federation (see also *And then Magnus created a chess club* by Jonathan Tisdall in New In Chess 2019/6). His stance in the gambling discussion wasn't appreciated by everyone and invoked considerable criticism. Remarkably, for the first time in quite some years, he was not on the shortlist of the most recent Sportsman of the Year awards, probably not because he lacked results. But then Michael Jordan didn't make his choices to please or curry favour either.

Interestingly enough, since Unibet is not allowed to operate in Norway, Carlsen cannot wear any branded clothing in his own country. But he can display his ties with Unibet when he is abroad, and those images will inevitably make their way into the Norwegian media.

Meanwhile, the World Champion has been expanding his business empire considerably: Play Magnus – of which he is a shareholder – has merged with Chess24 and acquired Chessable to become a real powerhouse (full disclosure: Interchess BV, the owner of New In Chess, is a very small shareholder in Play Magnus). The company is not yet making a profit, but investors' confidence is high. A share emission shortly before the start of the corona crisis brought in 13.5 million fresh dollars, and the Norwegian financial paper *Finansavisen* estimates the value of the company to be around 50 million US dollars. Carlsen used to be a major

CAITLIN O'HARA FOR THE NEW YORK TI

Danny Rensch, a founder of chess.com, preparing to offer commentary on the Online Nations Cup.

For Chess, New Normal Is Not a Problem

By DAVID WALDSTEIN

It was 8 a.m. Tuesday in St. Louis when the American chess grandmaster Fabiano Caruana,

hosting his own unique onlin event recently.

Carlsen won that event on Ma 3. When it was over, Jan Gustaf

The New York Times was only one of many media outlets that wrote extensively about the online chess boom.

shareholder, after the new emission he holds 16 per cent of the shares.

For the moment, their greatest rival on the internet is Chess.com, the biggest online platform in the world, and not surprisingly we saw their rivalry intensify during the recent online tournament bonanza. The Magnus Invitational had barely finished or Chess.com, in conjunction with FIDE, staged the Online Nations Cup.

Facts and figures

So, how big is the online chess boom really? Has there really been a sizable increase in fans following the live broadcasts? Going by the reactions from the major platforms, this is unmistakably the case. Daniel Rensch of Chess.com replied: 'We were pleasantly surprised with the amount of interest the Online Nations Cup garnered. Not only were we able to surpass viewership numbers from events like Tata Steel, we were also able to expand to twelve languages and bring on multiple broadcast partners across those languages.'

Leon Watson of Chess24 was also more than satisfied: 'The response has

been unbelievable. If anyone had said when the Candidates tournament started in March that within weeks an online event would totally eclipse that in terms of interest then no-one would have believed you. But it did.'

But did it bring Chess24 a substantial number of new Premium members, who could join with a nice discount during the Invitational? Watson: 'I can't tell you exact figures, but it was a big boost and

According to escharts.com, the largest public source of streaming analytics, the Magnus Invitational was watched at peak moments by around 110,000 viewers simultaneously

certainly helped us make the decision to put on the subsequent events we've announced and that have become the Magnus Carlsen Chess Tour. The fans have really spoken here and we count on their support for the future.'

And Rensch was similarly positive: 'It's always difficult to apply causality to events like the Online Nations Cup. The truth is, online chess is booming and there are multiple factors leading to its growth. Defining the funnel from external broadcast sources is a challenge but based on the responses we received from brand-new fans, we feel confident that the increased interest in this event led to an increase in new users.'

Still, the number of viewers were not in the millions, like FIDE tried to make us believe when they sent out press releases of the Nations Cup 'with an estimated audience of several million worldwide'. This, fortunately, is no longer the 600 million they liked to mention in the days of Kirsan Ilyumzhinov and of Agon/World Chess, but still a tad optimistic.

Likewise Watson stated: 'We believe chess from the Invitational was seen in around 10 million people's homes worldwide, either on TV or on the many, many internet streams. That is an incredible figure.' We agree. According to escharts.com, the largest public source of streaming analytics, the Magnus Invitational was watched at peak moments by around 110,000 viewers simultaneously (all languages and all platforms combined). In the case of the Nations Cup, this combined figure was around 50,000. It is not easy to see how, based on these numbers, you would be able to reach 10 million homes in the space of two weeks.

China

An unclear factor is the contingent of Chinese viewers, which is difficult to assess and is barely represented in the figures of escharts.com. For understandable reasons, e.g. the number of inhabitants, China is seen as a magical market for the near future, but how many really tune in? Rensch was impressed by the numbers he received: 'To use China as a prime example, we teamed up with China Sport & Leisure TV as well as CCTV and peaked at over 900,000 concurrent viewers during the final between Team USA and Team China. This event truly exceeded our expectations.'

FIDE press chief David Llada also believed that over a million Chinese watched the final rounds of the Nations Cup. Perhaps, but again it seems hard to believe that the interest in China is ten times that of the rest of the world combined.

Chess is rapidly growing in China, but it is mainly popular among children. Stories of children's tournaments who close entries once they have a thousand participants are not unusual. But we've seen few signs of such an immense popularity of the game otherwise. There may be an explanation for the high number of views in China, but it seems unlikely that it's the real number of fans that accounts for them.

Doubled

But of course there is no question that online chess has been thriving during the lockdown. You only have to look at the activity on Lichess, where the numbers have been soaring. Lichess is not a direct commercial rival of Chess.com and Chess24, since it is a free (and advertisement-free) non-profit platform that entirely depends on donations. But it's probably exactly for that reason that the two market leaders are closely watching this success story.

When we asked him about the impact of the corona crisis, Theo Wait of Lichess responded: 'The most illuminating figure here may come from looking at the numbers of those concurrently online. These figures track how many people have an open connection to Lichess. Our peak number of online users had been steadily increasing to just under 50,000 simultaneously online. Since mid-March, the peak has nearly doubled to just under 100,000 individuals simultaneously online. The average number of those online has

also increased dramatically. In the last 30 days, the average number of players online was 60,000. The average for February 2020 was 31,000.'

Part of the increased activity was caused by many teams and leagues, who could no longer meet physically, moving online to Lichess, e.g. 4NCL, the Bundesliga, La Liga, and even Magnus Carlsen's club, Offerspill. As a result, they had to scale up their infrastructure and, amongst other things, purchase a number of servers to handle the load.

'Next time at least triple'

With more than one platform trying to have the biggest part of the online pie, friction and controversy are hard to avoid. There is a fairly big pool of players that can attract a large audience, but no one comes close to Magnus Carlsen. He is the top draw – and automatically the biggest attraction Chess24 has. Not only as a player, but also as a commentator. No matter what you are watching on Chess24, you always have the feeling that he may break into the show and share his views, as if he is living in a room next-door to the studio.

For Chess.com it was disappointing that Carlsen had declined to play in the Nations Cup. Inevitably fans started asking for an explanation, possibly also because Chess.com had not really covered the Magnus Invitational as an important event. The official statement that followed was not well-received. The statement said that FIDE had dealt with the participants and that it was Chess.com's understanding that Carlsen had not accepted the same conditions as the other players. They added that they had the highest respect for him and would continue to invite him.'

The champ was not amused and tweeted: 'Thanks for putting up a very entertaining event, and letting me know that I will be invited to events in the future! Now that you have outed me as greedy, I will ask for

THE NEW EDITION OF GAME CHANGER WITH AN EXTRA CHAPTER ON COVID-19 WAS AN IMMEDIATE BESTSELLER

BEREND VONK

On his Twitch channel Hikaru Nakamura is exploring new horizons. His battle with former Overwatch professional xQc was not appreciated by all chess 'purists', but GMHikaru's army of fans and followers only keeps growing.

at least triple what I would have asked this time, though.' A typical Carlsen response, leaving them guessing about whether he was only being sarcastic or utterly serious.

Another Master of this Universe
Commercial interests also clearly played a role when Carlsen got embroiled in a controversy with Hikaru Nakamura. Among the top grandmasters, Nakamura is the most active streamer, and a very successful one. He has close to 300,000 followers on his Twitch channel and, perhaps even more importantly, more than ten thousand subscribers (both figures towards the end of May). They are paying various rates for various subscriptions, one of them is $5 per month – a nice source of extra income earned while explaining and commenting on games, playing against subscribers and other related activities.

On May 17, Nakamura proudly announced that he was the top English language streamer on Twitch, truly a most remarkable achievement if you consider that he has to compete with the most popular streamers of highly popular games like Fortnite.

Nakamura takes streaming seriously and decided to continue doing so while taking part in Magnus Carlsen's Tour. The champ criticized this, since he felt that it robbed the official broadcast of viewers. 'Naka' disagreed flat out, arguing that he only created more interest and exposure for the event, and soon a debate arose between two worlds: the serious chess lovers who follow the games on platforms like Chess24 ('elitists' in the eyes of many

Nakamura is one of the super-GMs and competes with the best, but at the same time he fully understands why the expert commentary on the leading websites is lost on many, or even most chess lovers

streamers) and the chess lovers who take things less seriously ('immature and loud' patzers in the eyes of the 'elitists'). The second group finds the Chess24 commentary 'inaccessible' and prefers to listen to streamers like xQc, who may not know much about chess but are very entertaining. Or Hikaru Nakamura, of course.

It's a fascinating debate and it's going to last for a while, and may well be an essential contribution to the current online boom. Nakamura's role cannot be underestimated. He is one of the super-GMs and competes with the best, but at the same time he fully understands why the expert commentary on the leading websites is lost on many, or even most chess lovers. His stream proves his point and may also teach us a lot about the way chess will go.

Something lacking
The coming months will also tell us when traditional tournaments will resume, because much as we are entertained by the current online events, they still feel like substitutes. There is something lacking, as in a football match without a crowd, as every player will tell you. FIDE wants to have the second part of the Candidates tournament as soon as possible, but nothing has been announced yet. If it's held in Yekaterinburg, we may have to exercise patience, since it is not certain that the corona crisis in Russia has reached its peak yet. More realistic is to hope that Magnus Carlsen will sit down again at a real board to play chess in Norway Chess, which is scheduled to start on October 3. And there are more traditional tournaments that are actively preparing their events while adjusting to the inevitable restrictions. The Tata Steel Chess tournament will inevitably be less crowded than usual, but the plan is to have the first round on January 16, in Wijk aan Zee. We can't wait. And while we're waiting, we'll enjoy the game online. ■

When the Host is the Winner

Magnus Carlsen initiates new chess normal with lucrative online event

Demonstrating leadership and business acumen, the World Champion gave a fresh impulse to the battered chess circuit. The Magnus Carlsen Invitational boasted a $250,000 prize-fund, including a $70,000 first prize. Needless to say who Carlsen regarded as the favourite for that one. And rightly so. **SIMEN AGDESTEIN** reports.

With much of daily life having come to a standstill due to Covid-19, and virtually the whole world stuck in self-isolation for the same reason, the Magnus Invitational came as welcome relief. Chess professionals and fans alike were longing for action, with all major 'classical' events cancelled or postponed. The World Champion took the initiative and Chess24 pulled out all the stops to bring the show to a global audience. The main broadcast was in English, but there was also a German, Spanish, French, Russian, Turkish, Portuguese, Chinese and even Norwegian channel, together serving an audience of over 100,000 viewers on the best days.

In fact, the Magnus Invitational turned out to be a kind of pilot. As Magnus himself said at the launch of the event: 'I can't disclose much yet, but I can say that there will be more tournaments like this. For everyone who wants to watch, this is not the end, but rather the beginning of something that will be a lot of fun in the future.' Only a few weeks later, the Magnus Carlsen Chess Tour was announced, with five more tournaments in the next few months, again with big prize funds. For the professionals invited this is great news, and equally so for everyone that loves seeing the very best in action.

Still, there is some food for thought here as well it turns out that more and more of the big events will be 'online only'. What about Norway Chess and other good old classical tournaments?

Is chess about to become just another online game like Fortnite or World of Warcraft? I guess there is a lot to be learnt from the gaming industry. The concept of banter chess, for instance, is just one thing that comes from e-sports, and seems to contribute to the popularity and accessibility of the game.

Whether we like it or not, we may be seeing a big shift for our dear game and the corona crisis may have added fuel to an inevitable(?) development. Suddenly there was no choice but to go online, and for many of us it probably didn't even make that much of a difference. Still, I hope that at some point life will return to more

'This is not the end, but rather the beginning of something that will be a lot of fun in the future'

As the host and most prominent participant, Magnus Carlsen was a frequent presence in the Chess24 broadcasts of the Magnus Carlsen Invitational. At even more frequent intervals the viewers were reminded that this was a good moment to go for Premium membership.

or less normal, and that we will also be able to meet over the chessboard again.

Sending out invitations

The format of the Magnus Carlsen Invitational very much bore Magnus's stamp, and he personally selected the participants. I don't know what criteria he applied, but those chosen must have been happy to be given a chance to win a minimum of 15,000 dollars and a top prize of 70,000. Inviting the next four in the world rating list – Fabiano Caruana, Ding Liren, Ian Nepomniachtchi and Maxime Vachier-Lagrave – was obvious. The other three – Hikaru Nakamura, Anish Giri and Alireza Firouzja – were upgraded and invited for different reasons. Firouzja had just beaten Magnus in the Banter Blitz Cup 2020, and is regarded by many as Magnus's main contender in the near future. Interestingly, Magnus gener-

ously talks him up and includes him, perhaps because he is eager to even the score.

The tournament concept was new. It started with all-play-all four-game matches, with the best four proceeding to the semi-finals. The format of 15 minutes per game plus 10-second increments made time a very important factor, while simultaneously giving the commentators enough space for interesting discussions. There were only two matches per day, which made it easier for the viewers to follow the entire event.

It surely was fun watching the show with all the time-scrambles and mistakes and, not least, the many decisive results. The quality obviously suffers with so little time compared to classical chess, which makes it hard to find great instructive games that will live on for ever. With this short time-control, the old search for perfection was replaced by a more practical

approach. Perhaps Magnus's win over Caruana came closest to a really well-played and instructive game that demonstrated the edge of the bishop over the knight.

Magnus Carlsen
Fabiano Caruana
MC Invitational prelim 2020 (3.2)
Queen's Gambit Accepted

1.d4 ♘f6 2.c4 e6 3.♘f3 d5 4.♘c3 dxc4 5.e3 a6 6.a4 c5 7.♗xc4 ♘c6 8.0-0 cxd4 9.exd4 ♗e7 10.♗e3 0-0 11.♘e5 ♗d7

12.♘xd7! Noting else gives much. **12...♕xd7 13.d5 exd5 14.♘xd5 ♘xd5 15.♕xd5 ♕xd5 16.♗xd5**

The interesting thing about the game is that even the computers give White a clear advantage. **16...♗f6 17.♖fd1 ♖fd8 18.♔f1 ♖d7** White would regain the b7-pawn if Black takes on b2. **19.♗f3 ♖ad8 20.♖xd7 ♖xd7**

21.♖c1! ♖d6 21...♗xb2 22.♗xc6 wins a pawn for White. **22.b4! g5 23.♖c5 ♘xb4** And finally, the b-pawns go. **24.♖c8+ ♖d8** 24...♔g7? 25.♗c5!. **25.♖xd8+ ♗xd8 26.♗xb7**

The game has turned into an instructive example of the strength of the

bishop pair. **26...♔g7 27.♔e2 a5 28.♔d2**

The white king cannot be stopped, since 28...♗f6 29.♗b6 loses the a-pawn. **28...f5 29.♔c3 ♔f6 30.♔c4 ♗c7 31.h3 g4 32.♔b5 ♔e5 33.hxg4 fxg4**

34.♗b6! ♔d6 35.♗xc7+ ♔xc7 36.♗e4! Very clean. The knight is dominated. **36...h5 37.♔xa5 ♘a2 38.g3 ♘c3 39.♗c2 ♘e2 40.♗g6** Black resigned.

The art of flagging

The matches took a few hours, but every second of the 16 days was filled with action. There were very few dull thinking pauses with nothing happening. The fighting spirit was fed further by every clean match win being awarded by three points. In case of a 2-2 tie, an Armageddon game decided whether the player got two points or one. Many matches went to the wire, and we saw some hard-core bullet time-scrambles, when it was all about 'flagging' while the clock was ticking down to zero. Alireza Firouzja is one of the toughest flaggers, closely followed by veteran

Hikaru Nakamura. Magnus also belongs to the generation that has played thousands of games online and of course handles this aspect of the game extremely well.

I wasn't surprised to see Magnus and Nakamura meet in the ultimate final, but as usual the margins were small. The two favourites had already met in the first round of the preliminaries, when White interestingly won in all five games. Magnus took home victory in the Armageddon. Chesswise, the most interesting aspect of that match was perhaps that Magnus managed to break Nakamura's deadsolid Queen's Gambit.

NOTES BY
Anish Giri

**Magnus Carlsen
Hikaru Nakamura**
MC Invitational prelim 2020 (1.1)
Queen's Gambit Declined, Blackburne Variation

1.d4 ♘f6 2.c4 e6 3.♘f3 d5 4.♘c3 ♗e7 5.♗f4 0-0 6.e3 ♘bd7

About once a year (usually when he has to win the last round in the US Championship as Black) we get to see the old Hikaru playing something sharp and risky, but Nakamura is all about solidity these days. This line is a perfect fit for someone who wants to be rock-solid. The alternatives are 6...c5 and 6...b6, but both of them demand far more concrete knowledge, and while Hikaru certainly has quite some knowledge there, remem-

About once a year (usually when he has to win the last round in the US Championship as Black) we get to see the old Hikaru playing something sharp and risky, but Nakamura is all about solidity these days

bering it on demand would be the main challenge.

7.c5

The most principled move, making sure Black will not break free with ...c7-c5 any time soon. A kind of lazy theoretical debate has been going on for a long time here, but without a clear verdict. Black is quite solid, of course, and usually holds, but if he does get in some trouble, he will face a long and tough defence.

7...c6

7...♘h5 was played later in the tournament by Carlsen, while 7...♘e4 is also around, but hasn't been played at the top level for a while.

8.h3

Very subtle; the point being that after 8...b6 9.b4 a5 10.a3 ♗a6 White can capture on a6 at once, compared to the old main move 8.♗d3, when the bishop would make two moves instead of one.

8...b6 9.b4 a5 10.a3 h6

Another fashionable finesse. The point once again is to wait for ♗d3 and only then go ...♗a6. Subtle stuff.

11. ♗d3 11.♕c1 is the way to continue the subtle waiting game.

11...♗b7?

This is totally ridiculous in combination with the move ...h7-h6. It would have been OK if Black had started with it instead of 10...h6, but after waiting for ♗d3, he should have gone ...♗a6 at once, of course.

Normally, a tempo more or less is not all that important in this set-up, but this one is actually quite crucial, as we will see later.

12.0-0 ♕c8 13.♖e1! ♗a6 14.♗c2!

White usually never gets time to keep the bishops like that. Black is always cramped, and the fact that there is an extra pair of bishops on the board makes his position practically unplayable. Black can't activate his rooks via the a-file here and White can prepare the dangerous e3-e4 push. With some minor adventures, Magnus eventually converted.

14...♖e8 15.♖c1 axb4 16.axb4 bxc5 17.bxc5 ♗d8 18.♖a1 ♗c7 19.♕d2 e5 20.dxe5

♘xe5 21.♘xe5 ♗xe5 22.♗xe5 ♖xe5 23.♕d4 ♖e8 24.e4 dxe4 25.♘xe4 ♘xe4 26.♖xe4 ♖d8 27.♕c3 ♖d5 28.♖ea4 ♗b7 29.♖xa8 ♗xa8 30.♕a5 ♗b7 31.♕b6 g6 32.♗e4 ♖d7 33.♗f3 h5 34.♖e1 ♕d8 35.♕xd8+ ♖xd8 36.♖e7

36...♗a6 37.♗xc6 ♖c8 38.♖e8+ ♖xe8 39.♗xe8 ♔f8 40.♗c6 h4 41.f4 ♔e7 42.♔f2 f6 43.♔e3 ♔e6 44.♗e4 g5 45.♔d4 gxf4 46.♗d5+ ♔e7 47.♔e4 ♗c8 48.♔xf4 ♗d7 49.g3 hxg3 50.♔xg3 ♔f8 51.h4 ♔g7 52.♔f4 ♔h6 53.♗f3 ♔g7 54.♔e4 ♗c6+ 55.♔e3 ♗b5 56.♔d4 ♔f7 57.♔d5 ♔e7 58.♗g4 ♗d3 59.c6 f5 60.♗f3 ♗b5 61.c7

61...♔d7 62.♔e5 f4 63.h5 ♗c4 64.h6 ♔g8 65.♔d5 ♗h7 66.♔e4 ♔g8 67.♔xf4

Black resigned.

■ ■ ■

Magnus won also the third game with the same opening. Nakamura obviously didn't repeat the same opening inaccuracy, but misplayed a completely drawn ending.

NOTES BY
Anish Giri

Magnus Carlsen
Hikaru Nakamura
MC Invitational prelim 2020 (1.3)
Queen's Gambit Declined, Blackburne Variation

1.d4 ♘f6 2.c4 e6 3.♘f3 d5 4.♘c3 ♗e7 5.♗f4 0-0 6.e3 ♘bd7 7.c5 c6 8.h3 b6 9.b4 a5 10.a3 h6 11.♗d3

11...♗a6 Hikaru looked up the theory during the break (although

I suspect he realized he had already mixed things up during the first game) and plays the main move.
12.0-0 12.♗xa6 ♖xa6 13.b5 is a constant theme in this line, with crazy complications.
12...♕c8 13.♕c2

White is ready to lose a tempo, but the position is very subtle and it is not clear how much these tempi matter, and, more importantly, whether a move like ♖b1 is actually useful.
13...♗xd3 14.♕xd3 ♕b7 15.♕c2 ♖fc8

16.♖fb1 Another common idea is to temporarily abandon the a-file and focus on the b- and c-files with ♖ab1/♖fc1. It is all pretty abstract.
16...axb4 17.axb4 ♗d8 A common plan – trading another pair of bishops. **18.♕c1 ♗c7 19.♖xa8 ♖xa8 20.♗xc7 ♕xc7 21.♖a1**

Magnus trades all the rooks as well. In fact, thanks to the weakness on c6, White is probably better in most endgames, but this is often not enough to win.
Famously, one needs two weaknesses for the principle of two weaknesses to work...
21...♕b7 22.♖a3 ♘e8 23.♘e2 ♖xa3 24.♕xa3 ♘c7 25.♘f4 ♕a6

Hikaru offers further trades.

Magnus Carlsen and Hikaru Nakamura played a total of 9 games of which White won 7! They both seemed amused that it was the first draw that finally decided the final in Carlsen's favour.

26.♕xa6

It is probably objectively stronger to keep the queens, but in a rapid game I can imagine that you don't want to allow Black any activity, and the queen on a6 seemed like it was about to jump in somewhere.

26...♘xa6 27.♘d3 f6

The knight ending looks pretty safe for Black, since White can't attack the c6-pawn even once for now; but the game continues.

28.♘d2 ♔f7 29.f4 ♘c7 30.♔f2 ♘b5 31.♔f3

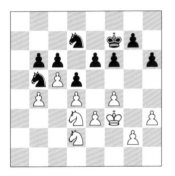

31...♘c3 This is quite cool – the knight jumps in!?

32.g4 g5 33.f5?!

Very ambitious, but actually not very good.

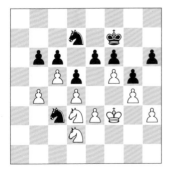

33...e5?!

33...exf5! 34.gxf5 b5 is bad news for White once he realizes that ...♘b8-a6 and ...♘a2 is a massive threat to the b4-pawn. And e4 can always be met by ...dxe4 ♘xe4 ♘d5!. White is in trouble here.

34.♘c1 e4+ 35.♔f2 ♔e7 36.♘f1 ♘a4 37.♔e2 ♘b2 38.♔d2 ♘c4+ 39.♔c3

39...♘b8

39...b5!? is a fortress: 40.♘b3 ♘b8 41.♘a5 ♘xa5 42.bxa5 ♘a6 43.♘g3 ♔f7 44.♘e2 ♔e7 45.♘c1 ♔d7, and there is no way White can enter or break through.

40.♘b3 ♘a6 41.cxb6!?

The game continues, and even though White is not better here, Hikaru suddenly cracks.

41...♘xb6 42.♘a5 ♔d7 43.♘g3

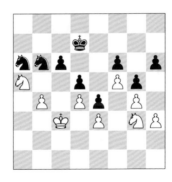

43...♔c7?

Hikaru wants to send the b6-knight to defend f6, but it would have been better to dispatch the a6-knight for this rather dishonourable job: 43...♘c7 44.♘h5 ♘e8, and this should be equal: 45.b5 cxb5 46.♔b4

Celeb 64

John Henderson

Greta Scacchi

There are celebrities who like to be photographed playing chess and some who pretend to play a good game. Screen siren Greta Scacchi not only likes chess, but her name literally *is* chess! Scacchi (pronounced 'Skacky') is the Italian-born, Australian-raised, and now London-dwelling Emmy-winning actor, who through the 80s and early 90s was one of the world's most desirable leading ladies. She won awards and critical acclaim for her Hollywood roles in films such as *Heat and Dust*, *White Mischief*, *Presumed Innocent* and *The Player*.

Over the years, Scacchi has lived up to her name with some notable chess cameos. The actress took a bigger interest in the game in 1988 when – after an intensive coaching session from four-time British Women's champion WGM Sheila Jackson – she agreed to play GM Matthew Sadler in a celebrity charity simultaneous to help raise money for Sports Aid.

After that, she admitted in media interviews that she loves to challenge family and friends and often plays on her name and celebrity associated with chess. The latest saw Scacchi adorn a London Underground billboard charity campaign, as she strategically sat beside her Staunton wooden chess set at home, as one of fifteen A-list celebrities supporting independent bookshops, while she read the Napoleonic epic *The Passion* by Jeanette Winterson. ∎

♘c4, when Black seems likely to hold in the end.
44.♘h5 ♘d7 45.♘b3

45...♔d8?
45...♔d6! 46.♘c5 ♘ab8 would still keep things together, although the knight on b8 is quite sad.
46.♘c5 ♘ab8 47.b5! cxb5 48.♔b4

And White breaks through and wins.
48...♘c6+ 49.♔xb5 ♘a7+ 50.♔a6 ♘xc5+ 51.♔xa7 ♘b3 52.♔b6 ♘d7 53.♘xf6+ ♔d6 54.♘e8+ ♔d7 55.♘c7 ♘xd4 56.exd4
Black resigned.

■ ■ ■

Altogether Nakamura played 10 games with this line and lost four of them. His only win was against Firouzja, but there, too, he was far worse. So we had a little opening discussion, but theoretically it doesn't seem as if White has made much progress in his attempts to break Black's solid set-up.

Caruana also made an attempt against Nakamura and came up with an interesting new idea.

NOTES BY
Anish Giri

Fabiano Caruana
Hikaru Nakamura
MC Invitational prelim 2020 (5.1)
Queen's Gambit Declined, Blackburne Variation

1.d4 ♘f6 2.c4 e6 3.♘f3 d5 4.♘c3 ♗e7 5.♗f4 0-0 6.e3 ♘bd7 7.c5 c6 8.h4!?

A fresh idea by Caruana. Similar to h3, but different. Food for thought!
8...b6 9.b4 a5 10.a3 ♘e4
An unusual way of dealing with the problems Black has to solve, but Hikaru probably thought that with the pawn on h4 potentially hanging, this makes sense here.
11.♘xe4 dxe4 12.♘e5 ♘xe5 13.♗xe5

13...♕d5
Obviously the pawn was not hanging, in view of ♕h5.
14.♗e2 ♗a6 15.0-0 ♗xe2 16.♕xe2 axb4 17.axb4 bxc5 18.bxc5 ♗xc5
Not wanting to stay passive and worried about the long-term

weakness of the c6-pawn, Hikaru simplifies everything. But the ensuing position remains tricky.

19.♗xg7! ♔xg7 20.dxc5 ♕e5 21.♖ad1

The position is more or less equal, due to the very limited material; but in practical chess, the difference between the kings' safety is striking, and eventually Fabiano wins quite nicely.
21...♖a5 22.♖d4 ♔h8 23.g3 ♖xc5 24.♖b1 ♖d5 25.♖c4 c5 26.♕c2

26...f5?
Chronically weakening the 7th rank. Black is now doomed to a passive defence.

26...♖fd8 27.♖xe4 ♕f5 would have been fine, as it is hard for White to coordinate his major pieces because of all the pins. If Black trades the queens, he should be able to hold the endgame.

27.♖a4 ♖fd8 28.♖b7 ♖5d7 29.♖a8 ♖xb7 30.♖xd8+ ♔g7 31.♔g2

The kind of move that underlines the essence of the position. Black can't touch the white king at all, nor can he bring his king to any kind of safety, and White is bound to get to the weak e6-pawn in the end.

31...♖c7 32.♕a4 ♕f6 33.♕e8 ♔h6 34.♖d6 ♔g7 35.♕b8 ♖f7 36.♖c6 ♖d7 37.♖c8 ♔h6 38.♖xc5 ♖g7 39.♖c6 ♖e7 40.♖c8 ♖f7 41.♖e8 ♖e7

42.♕d8 ♖f7 43.♕d6 ♔h5 44.♖xe6 ♕g7 45.♕f4 ♖f6 46.g4+ ♔xh4 47.g5+
Black resigned.

∎ ∎ ∎

Following this loss, Nakamura managed to level the score in this preliminary match, but in the Arma-

WHEN THE CLUB FINALLY REOPENED, MANY THINGS HAD CHANGED...

SERIOUS ?! SOCIAL DISTANCING NO LONGER ALLOWS TAKING EN PASSANT ?!

geddon game Caruana beat him again with the 5.♗f4 line. This time he didn't push 7.c5, but exchanged on d5.

Severely punished
As the preliminaries progressed, it soon became clear that there was a split field, with Magnus, Nakamura, Ding Liren and Caruana clearly ahead of the others. Since the exact final standings of the preliminary stage were of no consequence for the knock-out stage, Magnus was in an experimental mood in his last first-stage match. With essentially nothing at stake, he may have wanted to use the opportunity to try and humiliate Ding Liren with a couple of suspect openings: 1.e4 c5 2.♘f3 ♘c6 3.♗b5 h5!? and 1.e4 e5 2.f4!. Fortunately, one could say, he was severely punished. Magnus isn't *that* much better than the rest.

In the semi-final the next day, the same combatants met again. This time, Magnus obviously took things more seriously, but after an initial draw, he suddenly made a huge blunder:

Ding Liren
Magnus Carlsen
MC Invitational sf 2020 (1.2)

position after 31.♕d3

31...♔h7?? A very rare blunder by the World Champion. Black is a pawn up, but it seems as if White has enough compensation to keep the balance. This is far from obvious or easy to see, as the following computer line illustrates: 31...♘xe4!? 32.♖d8+ ♔h7 33.♘e3 ♖a4 34.f3 ♖a2+ 35.♔f1 (35.♔g1? ♕c1+ 36.♘f1 ♕c5+ 37.♘e3 f5 38.fxe4 ♖a3), and Black would be well-advised to take the draw with a perpetual. His ill-advised king move led to a rude awakening: **32.♖xf6 gxf6 33.♕e3** 1-0.

Things didn't look too good for the World Champion in the third game either. His opening had been highly suspect, but suddenly everything changed.

Magnus Carlsen
Ding Liren
MC Invitational sf 2020 (1.3)

position after 23.♖ce2

Ding had won a pawn in the opening, but Magnus had managed to create some nuisances on the kingside. **23...**

h6 23...f5 is anti-positional, but solid. The computer gives White enough compensation for an equal game. **24.f5 exf5?** It's surprising how fast it goes downhill from here. After either rook to e8, things are balanced, with chances for both sides. **25.♘h4 ♖ae8?** The problem is that this is not really possible. **26.♘xf5 ♗xf5 27.♖xe8**

27...♘d2!? A good try, but Magnus keeps his cool. **28.♖xf8+ ♔xf8**

29.♕xb7! ♘f3+ 30.♔h1 ♘xe1

31.♗xf5? How easy it is to point out mistakes with computer assistance! Surprisingly, this natural move gives Black the chance to recover. 31.♕a8+ ♔f7 32.♗xf5 is the correct move-order. **31...♘f3?** Ding misses 31...♕e7!, when suddenly it's not so clear. **32.♗g6** Now it's mate. **32...♘g5 33.♕c8+** 1-0.

The fourth game started slowly, but soon ended up in a mess.

Ding Liren
Magnus Carlsen
MC Invitational sf 2020 (1.4)

position after 25...♔h8

'Who's better and why,' as Jan Gustafsson kept saying. **26.♖f3!?** Blunder or bait? **26...♛g6** Magnus hesitates. **27.♖h3 ♛g5 28.♖f3** Magnus gets another chance, and this time he goes for it. **28...♘c3!? 29.d5 ♘xe2+ 30.♛xe2**

I think that neither the players nor the commentators, who were not using computers, and surely not the audience, who probably were watching a computer, understood what was going on here. **30...♗b7 31.♖g3 ♛h4 32.d6** 32.♘d6! is

Alexander Grischuk is a witness to the drama as Magnus Carlsen delivers the decisive blow in the semi-finals and Ding Liren understands what he has done.

completely winning, the machine says. One line is 32...♖xd6 33.dxe6 ♖e7 34.exd6 ♖xd6 35.♗xf5, and White's battery of bishops and major pieces soon breaks through. **32...♗e4 33.♗d1 ♗c6 34.♖h3 ♛g5 35.♖g3 ♛h4 36.♖h3 ♛g5**

37.♘c3? A brave but, in hindsight, stupid decision. Taking the draw with 37.♖g3 was advisable, but Ding must have thought he was much better and was looking for more. **37...♖f8** Taking on d6 is a necessity, and the sooner the better. After 37...♗xd6! Black suddenly has the most active pieces. **38.♛f2 ♛d8 39.♘e2 ♔h7** Again 39...♗xd6! was called for. **40.♘f4 ♗xd6** Finally, although a bit late, he takes.

41.♘xe6? A further mistake. After 41.exd6 ♖xd6 42.♗e2 White is well enough organized to maintain an edge. **41...♛e8 42.♘xf8+ ♗xf8 43.♛xf5+ g6**

Magnus Carlsen Invitational preliminaries 2020			1	2	3	4	5	6	7	8	TOTAL	POINTS
1 Hikaru Nakamura	USA	2736	*	2	2	2	2½	3½	2½	2	16½	15
2 Ding Liren	CHN	2791	2	*	3	2	2½	2½	2	2	16	15
3 Magnus Carlsen	NOR	2863	2	1	*	3	2	2½	1½	2½	14½	13
4 Fabiano Caruana	USA	2835	2	2	1	*	2½	3	1½	2½	14½	13
5 Ian Nepomniachtchi	RUS	2784	1½	1½	2	1½	*	2	2½	2	13	8
6 Alireza Firouzja	FRA	2728	½	1½	1½	1	2	*	2½	2½	11½	7
7 Anish Giri	NED	2764	1½	2	2½	2½	1½	1½	*	1	12½	7
8 Maxime Vachier-Lagrave	FRA	2778	2	2	1½	1½	2	1½	3	*	13½	6

44.♕f1? The final mistake. 44.♕c2 ♗e4! is tricky, but the hard-to-find 44.♕b1! solves all problems: 44...♗e4 45.♗c2 or 44...♖d2 45.♗f3, with an equal position either way. **44...♗g7?** It's very strange Magnus didn't immediately play the obvious 44...♖d2, with a double attack against b2 and g2.

45.♗c2? After 45.♖g3 anything could have happened, considering the quality of the previous moves. **45...♖d2!** Now, finally, it's all crystal clear. 0-1.

In this manner Magnus managed to get to the final – with games loaded with mistakes. We tried to get Peter Heine Nielsen, Magnus' main second, to annotate some of them, but he didn't find a single one he wanted to dig into. With a format like this, the beauty and artistic elements of chess suffers, while the sporting elements, like handling stressful situations with very little time and different psychological factors, come to the fore.

American duel

The other semi-final was an all-American battle between Caruana and Nakamura. After two draws Nakamura tightened the grip.

Fabiano Caruana
Hikaru Nakamura
MC Invitational sf 2020 (1.3)

position after 28...♗b6

Black is certainly better, but after 29.♖d1 ♖xa4 30.♗e6 White would fight on. Instead, Caruana ambitiously sends his rook to an awkward position. **29.♖e4 ♕f6 30.♖g4** 30.♖f4 g6 loses the bishop.

30...♖a5! In opposition to the white rook, Black's rook does an excellent job along the rank. **31.♗g6 ♗e6** Even stronger than taking on f2. **32.♘e4** The rook is trapped, since 32.♖e4 leaves the bishop on g6 unguarded. **32...♕xd4** White collapses. **33.♕xd4 ♗xd4 34.♖d1 ♗xb2 35.♖g3 ♗e5** and Nakamura easily converted his extra pawns (0-1, 41).

Miraculously, Caruana struck back in the next game from what looked like a horrible position to level the score and stay in the match.

Hikaru Nakamura
Fabiano Caruana
MC Invitational sf 2020 (1.4)

position after 23.♗d3

23...f4 It is hard to imagine Black coming first with the attack here, but it's even harder to come up with a reasonable alternative plan to the pawn push. **24.♘d5 ♘exd5 25.cxd5** Around this point, I stopped watching the show as I had to go out, and I could hardly believe my eyes when I came back later and found out that Caruana had managed to win this. **25...g5 26.♘c6 ♖e8 27.♔h1 g4**

28.♗h4 Nakamura is beginning to lose the thread. **28...♔h8** I wonder whether the players saw that 28... gxf3 29.gxf3 ♕h3 30.♕f2 ♗h5 was a highly relevant line here. It actually seems, however, that White is in control after 31.♗e2, since 31...♘xe4 32.fxe4 ♗xe2 33.♕xe2 ♕xh4 puts a stop to all Black's counterplay, whereas White's play on the queenside is just about to start rolling. **29.♗e2 ♗g6 30.♕e1 ♘h7 31.a4 ♘g5**

Magnus Carlsen watched Fabiano Caruana strike back in the all-American semi-final. It was not enough as Hikaru Nakamura prevailed in the blitz games.

Black is just in time with his counter-play. **47.♕d3** The e-pawn had to be defended. **47...h5!**

48.h4 There simply is no defence, and counterplay with 48.♖b1 is far too slow. Black comes first after 48...h4! (49.gxh4 ♗f4!). **48...♗xh4! 49.gxh4 ♕f6! 50.♔g1 ♕xh4 51.♕d2**

51...♔g6! Black can calmly include the king in the defence. **52.♘c4 ♕f6 53.♘a5 ♕h4 54.♘c4 ♕f6**

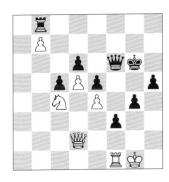

Of course, Caruana wouldn't repeat after 55.♘a5, but simply advance with 55...g3. **55.♘e3 ♕f4 56.♕f2 ♕xe4 57.♖e1 ♖xb7** There goes the last hope. **58.♘g2 ♕d4** 0-1.

32.♕f1? If you are worried, 32.♗xg5 hxg5 33.♖c4! kills all Black's play, but simply 32.a5 was also good enough. **32...♗f6**

33.a5? Suddenly, Nakamura is too confident and seems to have over-looked the simple threat. **33...♘xe4! 34.♗d3 ♗xh4 35.♗xe4 ♗xe4 36.fxe4 ♖f8**

37.b6 It's still not clear who is better. **37...axb6 38.axb6 ♕b7**

39.♖a1! ♖a8 39...♕xb6 40.♖db1 ♕c7 41.♖a7 loses the queen. **40.♖xa8 ♖xa8 41.♕b5 f3 42.g3 ♗g5 43.♘a5 ♕f7 44.b7 ♖b8**

Caruana is holding on on the queen-side. **45.♖f1 ♔g7 46.♕a6 ♕g6!**

In the first of two play-off blitz games, Nakamura quickly took the initiative and won a pawn, but eventually Caruana got his chance.

Fabiano Caruana
Hikaru Nakamura
MC Invitational sf 2020 (1.5)

position after 43.♖e8

43...♔h7? 44.♖b8? After 44.♕f3! White wins material and probably the game. Black cannot defend the knight, since 44...♘g6 45.♘g5+ wins the queen, while 44...♔g8 45.♕xf8+! is a knight down and 44...♘d7 45.♕h5 a mating attack. His best chance is 44...♕g6, but after 45.♖xe7! ♖xe7 46.♕xf8 White should win. **44...♘d7 45.♕d3 ♕g6 46.♖c8 ♘f8**

47.♖xc6?? It is perhaps a relief to see that even the very best can make big blunders, but also a bit sad that prestigious events are decided this way. **47...♕xc6 48.♘g5+ ♔h8** There is no mate on h7! **49.♘f7+ ♔g8 50.♘xe5 ♕d5 51.♗f4 ♗xc5** 0-1

Caruana now had to win the second play-off blitz game with Black, which turned out to be too much to ask.

Dream Final

And so the scene was set for the 'dream final' with perhaps the two best online players in the world. However, I think neither of them had much to boast about if we look at the quality of their play. Magnus won the first game when it seemed to be on course for a clear draw. However, with this format, if you play long enough, something will eventually happen. In the next game Nakamura fought back with a sweet endgame.

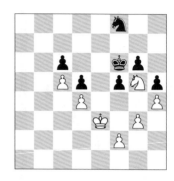

39...♘d7 It may be a topic for Karsten Müller's next endgame book to establish whether 39...♘e6 40.♘xe6

And so the scene was set for the 'dream final' with perhaps the two best online players in the world

Hikaru Nakamura
Magnus Carlsen
MC Invitational final 2020 (2)

position after 35.♕d3

For a change, Nakamura was White in this classical structure from the 5.♗f4-line of the Queen's Gambit. White is slightly better. Black needs to make some hard decisions, which of course is hard to do with so little time. **35...♕f5** This is OK and would happen anyway, since White soon will force it with f3. **36.♕xf5 exf5?** The computer says 'zero zero' after 36...gxf5!, but the lines are long and far from obvious. Black has a wonderful route for the knight on f8: g6 (threatening ...f5-f4 on the way)-e7-c8-a7-b5 and counterplay against d4. **37.♔f3 f6 38.exf6+ ♔xf6 39.♔e3**

♔xe6 is a draw. At first it seems very plain with 41.♔f4 ♔f6 42.f3, but Black has 42...g5!+, and it becomes a race after 43.hxg5 ♔g6 44.♔e5 ♔xg5 45.♔d6 f4. **40.♘f3** White could fix the decisive pawn structure at once with 40.f4!. **40...♔e6 41.♘e1 ♘b8 42.♘d3 ♔f6**

43.f4! Preventing ...g6-g5 and giving Black no counterplay. **43...♘d7 44.♘e5! ♘f8** 44...♘xe5 45.fxe5+ is clearly winning for White. **45.♘xc6** There goes the first pawn. **45...♔e6 46.♘e5 ♔e7 47.♔d3 ♔d8 48.♔c3 ♔c7 49.♘d3 ♘d7 50.♘b4 ♘f6 51.♔b3 ♔b7 52.♔a4 ♘e4** Black is lost anyway. **53.♘xd5 ♘xg3 54.♔b5 ♘e4 55.c6+ ♔c8 56.♔b6 ♘d6 57.♘e7+** 1-0.

After five white wins in the preliminary match between the same players and having started the final with another two white wins, Magnus managed to keep the rhythm and won again as White.

Magnus Carlsen
Hikaru Nakamura
MC Invitational final 2020 (3)
Queen's Gambit Declined, Blackburne Variation

1.d4 ♘f6 2.c4 e6 3.♘f3 d5 4.♘c3 ♗e7 5.♗f4 0-0 6.e3 ♘bd7 7.♗e2 dxc4 8.0-0 c5 9.dxc5 ♗xc5 10.♗xc4 a6 11.♘g5

11...b5!? 11...h6 was an alternative. **12.♗xe6!** Both players were probably aware of Wojtaszek-Andreikin from the Jerusalem GP some months ago, and both seemed to be happy with the lack of balance. **12...fxe6 13.♘xe6 ♕e7** Andreikin played 13...♕e8, which is recommended by the computers and makes one wonder how well acquainted Nakamura actually was with the line. **14.♘xf8 ♕xf8 15.♘e4 ♗b7 16.♘xc5 ♕xc5 17.♖c1 ♕d5**

18.f3!? It's interesting to see Magnus's character playing a part

in the way he plays chess. He is more interested in activity than in material. Trading queens is the most natural move. **18...♕xa2 19.e4 ♘f8 20.♖f2 ♖c8 21.♖xc8 ♗xc8 22.♕d8 ♕e6 23.♗d6 ♕e8**

24.♕xe8! Now it's time for trading. **24...♘xe8 25.♗b4 ♘e6 26.♖d2** The rook shows its superiority over the two pieces. **26...♔f7 27.♔f2 ♘f6 28.♔e3 g5 29.♖d6 ♘d7 30.g3 ♘e5 31.b3 h5 32.h4 gxh4 33.gxh4 ♘g6 34.♗e1**

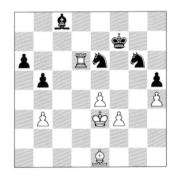

34...a5 Now all Black's pawns go, but White was threatening 35.♗g3 and pushing the f-pawn. **35.♖d5 a4 36.♖xh5 ♘ef4 37.♖g5 axb3 38.h5 ♘f8 39.♗c3 b4 40.♗b2 ♘8e6 41.♖f5+ ♔g8**

42.♖xf4! The simplest. **42...♘xf4 43.♔xf4 ♗a6 44.♔g5 ♗d3 45.♔g6 ♗b5 46.f4 ♗e8+ 47.♔g5 ♗c6 48.e5 ♗d5 49.f5 ♔h7 50.e6 ♗c4 51.♔f6 ♗e2 52.♔e7** 1-0.

Actually, in the fourth game Nakamura was close to continuing the 'White winning streak'. He won a pawn and managed to cling to it and reach a promising position.

Hikaru Nakamura
Magnus Carlsen
MC Invitational final 2020 (4)

position after 41.♘e5

41...♗xe5 Again, difficult decisions have to be made with very little time on the clock. **42.fxe5 ♔d7** Some computers say 42...g5, others say 42...♔d7. There are problems with both, but it's understandable that Magnus doesn't want his king to be driven back to the last rank.

43.♔g2? Here 43.h4! is absolutely necessary. White has good winning chances after 43...h6 44.a5 g5 45.h5!. **43...g5 44.♖d6+ ♔e7 45.♖a6**

♔d7 46.a5 h5 47.♖d6+ ♔e7 48.a6 h4

There are no more black pawn weaknesses on the kingside, and Black holds easily. **49.♖b6 ♔d7 50.♖d6+ ♔e7 51.h3 ♖a5 52.f4 g4 53.♖b6 ♖a2+ 54.♔h1 ♖a1+ 55.♔g2 ♖a2+ 56.♔f1 ♖a1+ 57.♔g2 ♖a2+** ½-½.

With this save, Magnus Carlsen won the final of the Magnus Carlsen Invitational 2½-1½ and added another 70,000 dollars to his bank account. Nakamura must have been pleased to pocket 45,000 dollar. The losers of the semi-final, Ding Liren and Caruana, got 30,000 dollar each, but all eight players were generously rewarded.

Magnus Carlsen Invitational 2020

Semi-Final	
Nakamura-Caruana	4-2
Carlsen-Ding Liren	2½-1½

Final	
Carlsen-Nakamura	2½-1½

	Prize money	
1	Magnus Carlsen	$70,000
2	Hikaru Nakamura	$45,000
3	Ding Liren	$30,000
	Fabiano Caruana	$30,000
5	Ian Nepomniachtchi	$22,500
6	Alireza Firouzja	$20,000
7	Anish Giri	$17,500
8	Maxime Vachier-Lagrave	$15,000

Highlight

It felt as if the quality of the games deteriorated a bit towards the end of the two tournament weeks. Perhaps the players got tired. As said above, it's not simple to find great games to dwell on, but Anish Giri's win against Magnus certainly was a highlight. Here are his notes to this game, which also include the game that Magnus won against Firouzja with the same line.

NOTES BY Anish Giri

Magnus Carlsen
Anish Giri
MC Invitational prelim 2020 (5.2)
Queen's Gambit Declined, Ragozin Variation

1.d4 ♘f6 2.c4 e6 3.♘f3 d5 4.♘c3 ♗b4 5.cxd5 exd5 6.♗f4

Magnus played this system against the Ragozin twice, against Firouzja and against me. Basically he would play it forever, until someone allowed him to show his 13.♖g1 novelty.
6...♘e4 7.♖c1 ♘c6 8.♘d2 g5 9.♗e3 ♘xc3 10.bxc3 ♗a3 11.♖b1 f5 12.g3

12...♗d6 An easy improvement over Firouzja's game, ready to meet f4 with capturing and ...♕h4+!. This had actually already been played before, in Gaehwiler-Georgiadis in 2019. 12...0-0?! was a rather natural mix-up by Alireza. The move is not bad either, but it allows f4!. Magnus continued 13.♕b3?!.

ANALYSIS DIAGRAM

It's not a great idea to include this, as Black gets a ...♘a5 tempo later on (13.f4! ♕e7 14.♗f2 ♗d6 15.♗g2 ♗e6 is very unclear actually, when White has a wide choice of options) 13...♗e7 14.f4 ♘a5! 15.♕c2 c6 (Black strengthens his d5-pawn) 16.♗g2 ♗d6 (16...g4!? doesn't look bad to me, stopping ♘f3-e5 once and for all. After 17.h3 h5, White can't really use the open h-file, while 17.c4 can always be met with 17...♗e6, 18.cxd5 cxd5, and Black holds the fort) 17.c4

ANALYSIS DIAGRAM

17...gxf4 (17...♕e7! is assessed as the best move by the computer, and, indeed, why not gain a tempo on the bishop?) 18.gxf4 ♗e6 19.cxd5 cxd5 20.0-0 ♔h8 21.♘f3 ♘c4 22.♕d3 b6 23.♔h1 ♕e7 24.♘e5

Hadn't we seen that shush sign before? Anish Giri clearly underperformed in the Magnus Carlsen Invitational, but found great satisfaction in his win against the host.

longer with check, and ...♕g2 mate comes first) 31.♗xf5 ♖g2.

ANALYSIS DIAGRAM

This doesn't work. 32.♗h3! (because this works for White – well calculated) 32...♖xe2 33.♕xe2 ♗xh3 34.♖g1,

ANALYSIS DIAGRAM

and Black resigned, since 34...♗g4 will be met by 35.♖fg3!, winning by pinning, Carlsen-Firouzja, MC Invitational prelim 2020 (2.1).
But let's return to our game.

13.♖g1!?
A peculiar novelty and a pretty deep one too. Now the obvious and critical response is 13...f4, winning a piece, but the ensuing position did not look

ANALYSIS DIAGRAM

24...♗xe5? (Black may not have played very accurately so far, but giving White the f4-square for the bishop is his first serious mistake) 25.fxe5 ♖g8 26.♗f4!.

ANALYSIS DIAGRAM

White's position starts looking nice, seeing that he can ignore

the c4-knight, while controlling all the entry points on the g-file. The f5-pawn is weak and Black's weakened dark squares on the kingside will start telling sooner or later. 26...♖g6 27.♗h3. Magnus goes after the f5-pawn and it works in the game, but it might have been less clear (27.♕h3! is an even better regrouping: 27...♖ag8 28.♗f3) 27...♖f8 28.♖f3 ♕h4 29.♖bf1 ♕h5 30.♗c1

ANALYSIS DIAGRAM

30...♖fg8? (Black tries to indirectly protect the f5-pawn, which he could have done with the sophisticated 30...♖f7!, when f5 is taboo in view of 31.♗xf5 ♗xf5 32.♖xf5 ♕g4!, and now the point of ... ♖f7 is revealed: the rook can still be captured but no

like the most practical choice. This being a rapid game, I didn't have much time to weigh all the options, but I did spend half of my time here to make sure the game would take a reasonable course.

13.♘f3 f4 14.♗c1 ♛f6 is how the Georgiadis game went (14...0-0! is not difficult to find as an improvement).

13...0-0!?

After this very natural move Magnus sank into thought. It is the unavoidable consequence of preparing with the computer that the most natural moves are dismissed if they don't enter the engine tab. No matter how much we (chess professionals) try to avoid this and analyse the human moves, they still slip away. No one is immune to this.

After 13...f4 14.gxf4 gxf4 15.♗xf4 ♗xf4 16.e3, 16...♛e7! is an important move to spot, but here it continues: 17.♛h5+ ♚d8 18.♛xd5+ ♗d6, when Black has won a piece for two pawns and has a reasonably stable position; but being unprepared, I didn't fancy the difference in my king's safety.

13...♛e7 is met by 14.♘f3, when the queen is somewhat misplaced on e7 and would rather be on f6.

13...♛f6 14.f4! gxf4 15.gxf4 ♛h4+ is a fat tempo for White, compared to 13.f4.

14.h4!

Nevertheless, Magnus found the best reply. To be honest, it didn't impinge on my radar when I played 13...0-0, and once I saw it, I immediately realized that it was the one, of course.

14.♘f3 can be met by 14...g4, or 14...h6 first, which was what I intended. 14.♛b3? was tempting, but here I had a strong reply ready: 14...♚h8!. 14.f4 was the most obvious move, but here I have 14...♛e7! 15.♗f2 ♘a5!?, with a very unclear position after 16.e3. Black doesn't have to fear ♘f3-e5 that much in view of the play on the light squares with ...♘c4, etc. Very messy.

14...f4!

The choice between 14...f4 and 14...g4 was a good test. I am glad I passed it. After 14...g4 15.♗g5 White's kingside structure is a rock, and White will break Black's centre with c4 sooner rather than later, so unless a miracle happens, Black is doomed.

15.gxf4 g4

With the king still on g8, this felt at the very least as dubious as it felt cool. In fact, while White has many interesting options, the position remains balanced, so surprisingly my reaction to the novelty seems to have been fine, even objectively.

16.♖b5?

This doesn't feel like the best practical decision, although it has some logic.

White wants to meet 16...♗xf4 with takes and e3/c4, while he intends to meet 16...♘e7 with the flashy 17.f5!?.

– 16.c4 felt very right. Here I saw the correct idea, but it is the engine that sees the correct execution: 16...♚h8!, keeping all options open: ...♗xf4, as well as ...♘b4 and ...♘e7 (16...♗f5, followed by ...♘b4, looks tempting, but the computer points out the flaw here: 17.♗g2!, when taking the exchange is a sin, with all the light squares gaping and it being unclear what ....♗f5 was for). 17.cxd5 ♘b4!?, when the position is insane but more or less balanced.

– 16.♗g2 is nicely met by 16...♘e7!, which is even stronger than capturing on f4 immediately.

– 16.♘f3 is also very testing, when after 16...♗xf4 17.♗xf4 ♖xf4 18.e3 ♖f7 19.c4 ♗g7 20.cxd5 ♛xd5 21.♘d2 ♚h8 Black's position looks strategically suspect. Black has lost the fight for the pawn centre, but White's potentially weak king ensures that he has adequate counterplay.

16...♘e7

Again, my choice wasn't too hard. One doesn't want White to rid himself of the ugly e3-bishop and give him easy play. Therefore 16...♗xf4 wasn't an attractive alternative.

17.f5!?

Spectacular and clever. Here I started feeling time-pressure a bit in view of the abundance of options, all of them very vague.

17...h5!?

Instead, 17...♘xf5 was the simplest, and pretty strong solution, but I wanted to have none of the ♖xd5xd6 sacrifice. 18.♖xg4+ (18.♗g5!? bothered me, but after 18...♕e8 19.♖xd5 ♕f7 the exchange sac is a fine version for Black, because he has kept his g4-pawn and gets a tempo, since f2 is hanging. Still very double-edged, of course) 18...♔h8 19.♗g5

ANALYSIS DIAGRAM

19...♘e3!!. It goes without saying that I didn't see this trick (19...♕e8 20.♖xd5 ♗e6 21.♖xd6 seemed like something I should really try to avoid) 20.♕b1!!. Stockfish says -0. 20. I'm outta here.

17...g3 is a flashy move which, combined with the fact that it was the first line of a weak engine on the website, prompted some people to ask me why I didn't play it. Many reasons, chief of which was that I didn't see how it was possible: 18.♗h6 ♘xf5 19.♗xf8 ♔xf8 20.♘f3 gxf2+ 21.♔xf2 ♗f4 22.♗h3

ANALYSIS DIAGRAM

with a mess; but one that is objectively balanced.
I also seriously considered 17...♔h8!?; I don't even remember why. But at some point I realized I should stop

with all the creative nonsense and just make a move.
18.♗g5 18.f6!? could transpose to the game, but not necessarily: 18...♖xf6 19.♗g5 ♖f5 (19...♕f8!? is another cool way to sac the exchange) 20.e4 ♖xg5 21.hxg5 c6 22.♖b2, and we've transposed to the game.

18...c6
Again, the time factor made me pick this one. I was very much into 18...♕e8 at this point, but this seemed more spirited and more direct.
18...♕e8!? 19.e4 (19.♗xe7 ♕xe7 20.♖xd5 ♗xf5) is total chaos: 19...c6 20.♖b2 ♘xf5 21.♕e2 and Black is doing quite well. He can, for example, sac a piece with 21...♕g6!?. although after the obvious 22.♔d1 the fight continues.
19.♖b2

19...♖xf5 Intending the exchange sac. 19...♗xf5!? seems to be strong:
– 20.e4! dxe4 21.♖xb7 ♖b8 22.♗c4+ ♔h8 23.♖xa7 ♕e8 24.♗h6, and Black can choose to repeat with 24...♖f6 or sac the exchange with, for example, 24...♗g6!?.
– 20.♖xb7 ♗c8 21.♖b2 ♕c7 is suddenly very good for Black. Indeed, the knight will go to g6, the bishop to f5 and

Black can take the b-file or break the g5-bishop by offering a trade. White's queenside is yet to be developed and his rook on g1 has no future, because trying to open the g-file with f3 will only backfire on his own king.
20.e4 ♖xg5! The point, otherwise the last five moves would have made no sense.
21.hxg5 Pre-moved. ☺
21...♘g6

I honestly had no idea how to evaluate this position in the heat of the battle, but I thought that, practically speaking, I was certainly very much in the game – which may have been overly modest in hindsight. White was, of course, less than thrilled having been forced on the back foot after unleashing a strong opening novelty.
22.e5 ♗f8
I was well aware of the fact that it is possible to spend half an hour here trying to choose between ...♗a3, ...♗c7, ...♗e7 and ...♗f8 (not sure ...♗b8 has some merit, but time can be spent thinking about that philosophical question, too). Enough is enough, however, and with the clock ticking I played this move instantly.

23.♗d3?!

This actually felt wrong, inviting 23...♘f4, but I suspect Magnus already had the ♘f1, f3 idea in mind at this point which, although positionally sound, has a minor tactical flaw.

23.c4 ♕xg5 24.♕b3 is natural, trying to get to the d5-pawn, although it is a little loose. Black has many interesting options, e.g. 24...♔h8!?, when White is better off trying to trade queens than actually grabbing that central pawn: 25.♕e3 (25.cxd5 cxd5 26.♕xd5 ♗f5, and with the a8-rook joining, Black will develop a very dangerous initiative).

My personal favourite here is 23.♘f3!, an absolutely sick move, offering the knight for just one pawn. Black, in fact, should ignore it: 23...b5 (23...gxf3 24.♕xf3 is simply very dangerous. ...♗g4 will be chopped off, too, and then White will invade on the weak light squares: 24...♗g4 25.♖xg4 hxg4 26.♕f5 ♕e8 27.♖xb7, etc.) 24.♗d3 ♘f4 25.♕d2!? (White insists on the piece sac) 25...♘xd3+ 26.♕xd3 gxf3 27.♕xf3 ♗g4 28.♖xg4 hxg4 29.♕xg4, and here the computer maintains the balance, thanks to the ...b4!? idea, with counterplay, but I would take White any day: 29...♕c8 30.e6 b4 31.cxb4 ♖b8.

23...♘f4! 24.♘f1 ♕xg5

25.f3??

This blunder is in a way the logical consequence of White's play, but it would still have made some sense if he had first withdrawn the d3-bishop to b1.

25.♘e3 b5 is good for Black, who is now in time with ...a5, ...♖a7 (25...♗a3!? 26.♖b3 ♗c1! is another strong resource. Also cool).

25.♗b1!? was best: 25...♘h3. Just one of the moves. The engine also suggests activating the bishop with ...♗h6 or ...♗a3 (25...b5 26.f3 a5 27.fxg4 ♖a7 is mayhem. If I had seen this idea, I would probably have been tempted to go for it) 26.♖h1 ♗h6 27.♘e3 g3 28.♕f3 ♘xf2 29.♖xf2 gxf2+ 30.♔xf2 ♗g4 31.♘xg4 hxg4 32.♕d3 ♕d2+ 33.♕xd2 ♗xd2

ANALYSIS DIAGRAM

This is one of the random ways in which the computer makes sense of this position. Here White ends up a pawn down, but should hold, because his position overall is good.

25...♘xd3+! 26.♕xd3 ♕c1+ 27.♔f2 ♕xb2+ 28.♘d2 ♗f5

In the heat of the battle I didn't immediately realize how completely winning this is, but when I saw that the incoming check on g6 was just a check, it immediately became clear.

29.♕xf5 ♕xd2+ 30.♔g3 ♕xc3

It may look as if a perpetual is on the cards, but White only has two checks, regardless of whether he starts from e6 or from g6, so he is dead lost here.

31.♔h4 ♕xd4 32.♖g3 ♗g7 33.f4 ♖f8 White resigned.

■ ■ ■

Crown Prince

It may be a burden to be dubbed 'crown prince', but if Alireza Firouzja actually wants to become a World Champion contender, he has to handle pressure better than he did in the loss to Magnus that Anish included.

Anyway, getting a chance to play Magnus and the world elite at the early age of 16 sounds useful, as long as you don't get busted. The young Iranian was struggling at the start, but match victories against Anish Giri and Maxime Vachier-Lagrave secured him sixth place. Beating Magnus also must have been nice, although the game wasn't very clear-cut.

Alireza Firouzja
Magnus Carlsen
MC Invitational prelim 2020 (2.2)

position after 39.♘f2

After he had expressed his delight about his match victory against Alireza Firouzja, Magnus Carlsen didn't mind explaining what had gone wrong in Game 2.

39...♖d2?? Magnus walks into a lethal mating net. **40.♖b8+ ♔h7 41.♕g4!** There is no defence against 42.♕g6+!. **41...♕f1+ 42.♖g2 ♕xg2+ 43.♔xg2** 1-0.

In his first game against Nakamura, Firouzja was surprised by an unfortunate technical issue that interrupted the game when he was in a seemingly winning position.

Alireza Firouzja
Hikaru Nakamura
MC Invitational prelim 2020 (3.1)

position after 45...♖b2

At this point, to the surprise of both the online viewers and himself, Firouzja's time ran out. There was no serious time-trouble. Since we could see the players on their screens, it was obvious that Firouzja thought everything was fine, but his move simply hadn't come through. Nakamura shook his head, waved his hands and left the computer, which made it hard to continue the game. A draw became the compromise solution. White is much better after 46.♔g3, walking away from the

Getting a chance to play Magnus and the world elite at the early age of 16 sounds useful, as long as you don't get busted

checks with the king. Black's problem is 46...♖xc7 47.dxc7 ♖c2 48.♖a7 ♔g6 49.c8♕ and mate on g7.

Nakamura won the next two games, but, for entertainment's sake, the fourth game had to be played as well. However, the show didn't last long.

Hikaru Nakamura
Alireza Firouzja
MC Invitational prelim 2020 (3.4)
Scandinavian Defence

1.e4 d5 2.exd5 ♕xd5 3.♘c3 ♕a5 4.b4!? With nothing at stake it's easy to have some fun. **4...♕xb4 5.♖b1 ♕d6 6.d4 ♕d8 7.♗c4 ♘f6 8.♘f3 e6 9.0-0 ♗e7 10.♘e5 0-0 11.♖e1**

11...c5? Keeping the position closed would have been better. **12.d5 exd5 13.♘xd5 ♗e6?**

14.♘xf7! ♔xf7 15.♖xe6 ♔xe6 16.♘xf6+ ♔xf6 17.♕f3+ ♔e5 18.♕g3+ ♔d4 19.♗b2+ And before he got mated, Black resigned. Perhaps this rare miniature will be saved by the historians as a curiosity. ∎

When the truth is somewhat different

Timman-Short, KRO-match 1989, Game 1 revisited

He loves old books. But how often, **NIGEL SHORT** wonders, are these 'original sources' misleading, incomplete, or plain wrong?

A few weeks ago, I was delighted to receive a parcel from the renowned historian Edward Winter containing five biographies/games collections, of yours truly, which I did not previously possess. To be frank, the publications, from Spain, Argentina, USA, Hungary and Germany, could not, in any way, be described as towering works of literature – being for the most part flimsy assemblages of lightly and even (horror of horrors) unannotated duels. Only *So Spielt Nigel Short* (Sportverlag Berlin, 1993) by Stefan Löffler, with Rainer Knaak, was a title of any substance, having both informative text, and an insightful selection of games. Indeed, I might even make use of it when lecturing in future...

Notwithstanding the technical and artistic deficiencies of the above books/pamphlets, it is a joy to receive such an act of generosity. They go particularly well on my shelves alongside the 8 or 9 other volumes that I already owned. And this being a plague year, when people are more conscious of their own mortality than usual, prompted a period of introspection.

After the biographies, I then proceeded to dust off no less than eight books on my 1993 World Championship with Garry Kasparov (a couple of others also exist, I believe) before moving on to lesser known matches. The booklet on the Timman-Short 'KRO Schaaktweekamp' 1989 in particular caught my eye.

With hindsight, this exhibition match, which ended in a 3-3 tie, proved to be a dress-rehearsal for the Candidates Final, a little over three years later. Both Jan and I were near our respective peaks and the games were highly entertaining, arguably because they were not particularly accurate.

A bottle of Glenlivet

After going down 2½-½ before the free day, I took solace, on that evening of leisure, in a bottle of Glenlivet, at the home of our esteemed editor, Dirk Jan ten Geuzendam. I had originally intended to return to my hotel, but by the end of the night was in no condition to accomplish so complicated a task, and ended up 'sleeping' – if such a word may be stretched to describe drifting in and out of a coma – on the most extraordinarily uncomfortable inflatable lilo.

I awoke, aching all over, with the mother of all hangovers, to take the train back to Hilversum. A brief rest brought no respite, for after 20 moves of the fourth game, I was totally busted, in horrendous time-trouble, and with the worst headache known to mankind. Perhaps Dionysos, in empathy, came to my aid, because, by a miracle, I won this game, just half a dozen moves later.

I won the next, in combative style, and even had good chances to take the match in the last.

Game One reviewed

In the match book, the first game was analysed by Paul van der Sterren and his comments are in quotation marks. The translations, from the Dutch, are by my son, Nicholas Darwin Short. The book prompted my review and as thus forms the foundation of these annotations, but it would be a little

In an act of chivalry, bravado, or astonishing stupidity (OK – the latter), I agreed to do so, provided he did not examine the variation in advance!

The 1989 KRO match between Jan Timman and Nigel Short received wide attention in the Dutch press and every day hundreds of fans visited the KRO studios in Hilversum to watch the two rivals in action.

enough – White stands a bit better. But, as will soon become patently clear, both the annotator and – more importantly – my opponent seriously underestimated the dynamic potential of the black position.

12.♖c1! 'Hjartarson played 12.e4, but after 12...♕a8, his centre wasn't very solid.' A rickety central edifice, indeed – the Icelander already stood worse after this premature advance. **12...♕a8 13.♘e1**

13...♘b8
'It would be exaggerated enthusiasm to call this the point of Black's construction, but it is logical. After 13...♘b4 14.♗xb4 ♗xb4 15.♗xb7 ♕xb7 16.♘d3 ♗d6 17.♘d2 Black never returns to the important advance ...c7-c5.'

14.♗a5 Neither side appreciated the importance of interpolating the accurate 14.♗xb7!, which, as his knight is closer to d3, gives White an edge. Timman's idea, however, is characteristically more ambitious – to make use of the b6-square and thereby win a pawn!

14...♖c8 Missing the opportunity to play 14...♗xg2!.

perverse not to incorporate some of Jan Timman's never dull contemporary comments from New In Chess 1990/2.

Jan Timman
Nigel Short
Hilversum 1989 (KRO match-1)
Catalan Opening
1.d4 ♘f6 2.c4 e6 3.♘f3 d5 4.g3

'Early in November 1989, in Lucerne, Timman chose 4.♘c3 against Short. Presumably he prefers the Catalan now, hoping that his opponent

chooses the dubious variation that will indeed appear on the board.'
There is an amusing story to this (see below), which I had completely forgotten. Once you know it, Timman's powers of prescience appear less impressive.
4...♗e7 5.♗g2 0-0 6.0-0 dxc4 7.♕c2 a6 8.♕xc4 b5 9.♕c2 ♗b7 10.♗d2 ♘c6 11.e3 ♖a7
'Short had played this with success against Hjartarson in Belgrade shortly before, but Timman shows its artificiality with some logical positional moves.'
In fact, as Timman related in his notes in New In Chess 1990/2, he had dared me – or rather goaded me – while in Yugoslavia, into trying the same line against him, on the next occasion we faced each other. In an act of chivalry, bravado, or astonishing stupidity (OK – the latter), I agreed to do so, provided he did not examine the variation in advance! What a naive idiot I was! Van der Sterren's evaluation is fair

15.♘d2

And once again spurning 15.♗xb7!. Timman mentions 15.♗b6 ♗xg2 16.♘xg2 ♖b7 17.♗c5 ♗xc5 18.♕xc5 c6 as being 'somewhat better for White'. It isn't. He lags in development and is unable to prevent the ...c5 break.

15...♗xg2 16.♘xg2

16...c5 'After the obvious 16...♘bd7 comes 17.♕c6 and the c-pawn is mercilessly captured. Without ...c7-c5 there is no coherence in the black position. A courageous pawn sacrifice, but also a clear sign that something went wrong for Black.'

It should perhaps also be mentioned, en passant, that 16...♘fd7 17.b4 e5 is playable – albeit a tad passive – and only slightly better for White.

17.♗b6 ♖d7 18.♗xc5 a5

19.a4 'A logical strategy: the pawn on a5 is fixed as a point of attack. Yet also 19.a3 a4 20.b4 axb3 21.♘xb3 came into consideration. Also, in that case the white chances are excellent.' Agreed. This is an important moment. The precise 19.a3! leaves White on top. After the text, however, the c5-bishop comes under fierce assault, which will require all his resources to maintain it.

19...b4

20.♘f4

A more challenging continuation is 20.♘b3!? ♘a6 (20...♘e4 21.♕e2!) 21.♕e2 ♘xc5 22.♘xc5 ♗xc5 23.♖xc5 ♖xc5 24.dxc5 ♘e4 25.♕b5!, but even here White struggles to prove any advantage against accurate defence, e.g. 25...♖b7 26.♕c6 ♖b8 27.♕xa8 ♖xa8 28.♖c1 ♖c8 29.c6 ♘d2 30.♘f4 ♘b3 31.♖c4 ♔f8 32.e4 ♔e7 33.e5 ♘d2 34.♖c5 ♘b3 and, despite the far-flung extra pawn, Black's activity is enough to hold the balance.

20...♖dc7

20...♗xc5 is a comfortable equaliser, e.g. 21.♘d3 ♘a6 22.♘b3 ♘e4 23.♘dxc5 ♘axc5 24.dxc5 ♖dc7 25.h4 h6 26.♕c4 ♘xc5 27.♘xc5 ♕a7.

21.♘d3 ♘bd7 22.♕c4 h5!

'Black tries to complicate the position. With the text-move he creates a field of refuge for his king and forces White to slightly weaken his king's position.'

Van der Sterren was on point. Curiously, though, Timman awarded this move a question mark, arguing that the inclusion of h4 and h5 was to White's advantage, as the g5-square is denied to a black knight. This heterodox view arises from the misconception that the white king can defend itself and that he therefore holds the advantage. However, as Timman diverts ever more resources to shoring up his bishop, the fallibility of his defences is tested.

23.h4 e5

Dubious, according to Van der Sterren. 'Abandoning the exchange on c5, Black puts everything in one basket. The crisis is approaching.'

The basket is, in fact, a highly promising one, and with this advance Black undermines the c5-bishop.

24.♘b3

24...♘e4

24...♘g4! was the best, after which Black already stood better, e.g. 25.♖c2 g5! 26.hxg5 ♗xg5 with rich counter-play. The white forces are far from the defence.

Also, 24...♕f3!? was a reasonable alternative.

25.♕b5?

Passed over without comment by Van der Sterren. The narrative thus far has been that with clever prepa-ration and logical positional moves, the Dutch titan has refuted the unre-liable, experimental opening of the upstart Englishman.

The objective truth, however, is somewhat different: Black is completely winning. Indeed 25.♕b5? is a typical psychological error of the eternally optimistic GM – and one that has brought him many more points than it has cost over the years. Someone with a heightened sense of danger – perhaps Ulf Andersson, say – would play 25.♕c2, scurrying to the defence of his king, after which c5 would fall in short order, and equality, and most likely a dull draw would ensue.

25...♘dxc5?

This knight is needed for the attack! Here 25...♘xg3!

ANALYSIS DIAGRAM

The narrative thus far has been that with clever preparation and logical positional moves, the Dutch titan has refuted the unreliable, experimental opening of the upstart Englishman

immediately is devastating: 26.fxg3 ♕f3 and now:
– 27.♘f2! ♕xg3+ 28.♔f1 ♗xh4 29.♕e2.

ANALYSIS DIAGRAM

It is important to spend a few minutes to take stock here. Black has only two pieces in the attack and, at first sight, White may appear to have beaten off the assault. In reality, it is merely a question of Black introducing rein-forcements before the defences are breached: 29...♖c6! 30.♗d6! (cunningly preventing 30...♖f6)

ANALYSIS DIAGRAM

30...♕g6!! (penetration is not to be denied!) 31.dxe5 (alternatively, 31.♗xe5 ♘xe5 32.dxe5 ♖c2 33.♖xc2 ♖xc2 34.♘d2 ♕f5 35.♖d1 ♖xb2 leaves White hog-tied and helpless) 31...♗xf2 32.♔xf2 (32.♕xf2 ♕d3+ wins) 32...♖c2 33.♖xc2 ♖xc2 34.♘d2 ♘b6! and White will shortly be overwhelmed.

– The main point is that 27.♗xe7? ♖c2! leads to instant catastrophe.

ANALYSIS DIAGRAM (after 26..♕f3)

– The defensive manoeuvre applied in the game fails here, e.g. 27.♔h2 ♘f6! (this is why this knight should not be exchanged) 28.♘xe5 ♕f2+ 29.♔h1 (29.♔h3? g5! 30.hxg5 ♘e4 mates) 29...♘e4 30.♖g1 ♕xb2 leaves White unable to cope with the combined threats of ...♘f2+ and ...♕xb3 (31.♖ab1 ♘xg3+!).

26.♘dxc5

'Especially not with the other knight: 26.♘bxc5? ♘d6 27.♕a6 ♖a7 28.♕b6 ♖c6 and the white queen is captured!'

26...♘xg3

'The only chance and at first sight also very dangerous for White. However, with a few sober moves Timman turns out to be able to defend everything.'
Or, as Timman would have it, 'A desperate sacrifice which turns out to be losing.'

Not quite. The sacrifice is still good enough for a draw.
27.fxg3 ♕f3 28.♔h2! ♕f2+ 29.♔h3

29...♗xh4? Only this tempting move loses. 29...g5! 30.hxg5 h4 31.♖g1 (31.gxh4 is very risky: 31...♕f3+ 32.♔h2 exd4 intending 33...♗d6+) 31...♕f5+ 32.♔h2 ♗xc5 33.♘xc5 exd4 34.exd4 hxg3+ 35.♖xg3 ♕f2+ 36.♔h3 ♕f5+

ANALYSIS DIAGRAM

and White cannot escape a perpetual without letting his d-pawn fall, after which he would need to be careful to maintain the balance, e.g. 37.♔g2 ♕d5+ 38.♔h2 ♕xd4 39.♘d3 ♖c2+ 40.♖g2. But why take serious and unnecessary risks?

30.♖g1!
'Bringing the black attack to a halt. A second sacrifice with 30...g5 doesn't give any significant odds. After 31.♖af1 g4+ 32.♔xh4 ♕h2+ 33.♔g5 ♖c6 34.♘e4 ♖g6+ 35.♔f5 Black doesn't come any further.'
30...♗g5 'Now the momentum is lost and White can consolidate.'
31.♖gf1 Certainly good enough, but 31.♖af1! is even better.
31...♕xb2

32.♖ab1
'Timman chooses a forcing variation, which is certainly sufficient for the win. However, even stronger was 32.♕d3, after which Black has no chances at all.'
Timman differs in his assessment saying that after 32.♕d3 ♕c3! 'I do not think White can win.'
I am not sure I would be so optimistic, although Black does have real practical chances to save the game.
Best, however, is the ice-cold 32.♖ae1!, which snuffs out all hope.
32...♕c2 33.♕d3

33...♖xc5? Another blunder. 33...♕xd3 34.♘xd3 exd4 35.exd4 ♖c3 still provided some resistance.

A race of 500 metres on exercise bikes was part of the drawing of lots of the 1992 VSB tournament in Amsterdam. Short clocked 42 seconds, beating Timman by one second.

34.♘xc5 ♖xc5 35.♕f5!

'Seems to win immediately, but Black still has surprisingly many chances of drawing.'
Only if White goes wrong!
35...exd4 36.♕xf7+ ♔h7

37.♖bc1?

Harshly, but probably correctly, given a question mark.
'Tempting, but not good. Much stronger was 37.exd4!, and after 37...♖c6, 38.♕f5+ leads to a won endgame.'
Indeed, after 38...♔h6 39.♕xc2 ♖xc2 40.d5 it is hard to believe that Black can survive.
37...♕xc1 38.♖xc1 ♖xc1

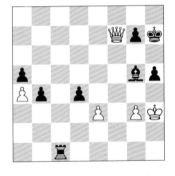

39.exd4

'It's surprising how great Black's drawing chances have suddenly become. The strong passed pawn on b4 is the big problem for White. The obvious 39.♕xh5+ doesn't work. After 39...♗h6 White has no time for 40.exd4 because of 40...♖h1+. And 40.♕xa5 b3 41.♕b5 dxe3 42.♕xb3 g6 leads to a draw. The two passed pawns will eventually be exchanged for each other.'
One may improve this variation with 41.♕d2!, but even in the best case scenario, after 41...♖h1+ 42.♔g2 ♖g1+! 43.♔f3 g6 44.♕b2 d3 45.♔f2 ♖h1 46.♕xb3 ♖a1! White will still have the formidable technical

obstacle to overcome in lifting the blockade on e5 after the inevitable exchange of the a- and d-pawns.
39...♔h6 40.♕e6+ ♗f6

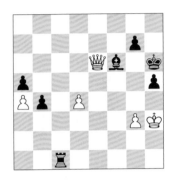

'The end of an exciting time-trouble phase. Black turns out to have just enough chances in this endgame.'
Yes, he does.
41.♕e3+ ♗g5 42.♕e5 ♖c3 43.♕xa5 h4?

'Too subtle was 43...♗f4. After 44.♕b6+ ♔g5 45.♔g2 ♖xg3+ 46.♔f2 b3 47.a5 the a-pawn decides.'
Timman passed over this critical moment without comment. In the above variation the obvious 44...g6! is good enough to draw.
44.♕xb4 ♖xg3+ 45.♔h2 ♖d3

'Tempting is 45...♗f4, but White has the strong answer 46.♕f8, after which he can't maintain his attacking battery properly. After the text move, Black's h-pawn – in combination with rook, bishop and possibly the king – forms a tricky threat to White.'
If I recall, although my memory is unreliable, particularly after all these decades, I had simply missed 46.♕f8, but perhaps it was worth going for it anyway, punting 46...♔g5, with fingers crossed.

46.♕d6+?!

The position defies easy human comprehension. 46.a5! appears highly risky, but after 46...♗f4+ 47.♔h1 h3 48.♕e1! Black is surprisingly unable either to create sufficient threats or erect a fortress. That said, even after the following sequence 48...g5 49.a6 ♖a3 50.♕e6+ ♔h5 51.♕e8+ ♔g4 52.♕e2+ ♔g3 53.♕h2+ ♔h4 54.♕f2+ ♔g3 55.♕f1, where my engine screams +48, victory is still not trivial. No wonder my antagonist couldn't find it over the board.

46...♔h5 47.a5 ♖d2+ 48.♔h3 ♖d3+ 49.♔h2 ♖d2+ 50.♔h1 ♖d1+ 51.♔g2 ♖d2+ 52.♔f3 h3!

This advanced passed pawn ought now to be amply sufficient to guarantee the draw.

53.♕c6

'An ingenious way to stop the h-pawn and with astonishing success, because suddenly Short seems to completely lose the plot.'

Damned right I did.

53...♖d3+?

'The first step on the way to a helpmate. With 53...h2 54.♔g3 ♖a2 Black would have the draw within reach. He can potentially exchange his h-pawn for the a-pawn, because the remaining endgame can't be won by White.'

The toll of playing a tense game for six hours begins to tell, because this is otherwise an inexplicable error. Incidentally, 54...♗h4+ 55.♔h3 ♗f6 is even easier.

54.♔e4

54...♖a3? The final mistake. Even here 54...♖d2 followed by ...h2 is still totally drawn.

55.♔f5!

'Simple and elegant. Suddenly the black king is hopelessly entangled in a mating net.'

55...♖xa5+ 56.d5 ♗f6 57.♕e8+

Black resigned. After 57...♔h4, 58.♕e1+ forks king and rook.

Conclusion

Of course, it is a trifle unfair, more than 30 years later, with a powerful engine at my fingertips, to tear through the cobwebbed musings of Paul van der Sterren. He is not the worst analyst by any stretch of the imagination: on the contrary, rather diligent and conscientious, as can be observed from his warmly recommended autobiography *Zwart op Wit*, and he can be certainly forgiven a little bias towards a national icon. But it makes one wonder just how often, when we sit down to enjoy an old book, is the narrative misleading, incomplete, or plain wrong on a matter of substance? It is hard to know the answer, but one suspects 'rather frequently'. ■

NEW FRITZTRAINER DVDs

Discover new ideas in the Benoni with Caruana's second, opening expert Rustam Kasimdzhanov.

Follow Erwin l'Ami who guides you through the fascinating lines of the Benko Gambit.

Or let Daniel King inspire you to try the King's Gambit!

ERWIN L'AMI:
THE BENKO GAMBIT EXPLAINED

Pal Benko left the world of chess an enormous legacy. Not only was he a formidable study composer, he also gave his name to the gambit line 1.d4 Nf6 2.c4 c5 3.d5 b5. In this DVD, Erwin l'Ami guides you through the fascinating Benko Gambit. As early as move three Black starts a fight for the initiative, a strategy that has proved to be successful in countless amateur and master level games. Through model games l'Ami explains all topical lines of the Benko Gambit, occasionally asking the viewer interactive questions that help the viewer to grasp the ideas behind this opening. The exercises on this DVD will also surely be of help. Many top players followed in Benko's footsteps, most notably Garry Kasparov, Veselin Topalov, and Magnus Carlsen. Will you be next? Video running time: 6 hours 30 min.

29,90 €

RUSTAM KASIMDZHANOV:
THE BENONI IS BACK IN BUSINESS

On top level, the Benoni is a rarer guest but with this DVD Rustam Kasimdzhanov, opening expert and second and coach of Fabiano Caruana, will turn the tables. New ways and approaches in most lines and countless improvements of official theory will show you how to play this opening at any level

with success. His preferred move order into the Benoni arises through 1.d4 Nf6 2.c4 e6 3.Nf3 c5 which complements his already published DVD on the Nimzoindian. Kasimdzhanov goes into extreme detail, showing that the Benoni is a reliable opening that often leads to truly fascinating positions. You'll be able to practice the lines shown in the Opening Trainer and you can play key positions to improve your understanding of typical structures and patterns of the Benoni.

29,90 €

DANIEL KING: POWERPLAY 27 –
THE KING'S GAMBIT

Glorious sacrifices, unexpected tactics and checkmating attacks. The King's Gambit is one of the oldest and most romantic openings in the game of chess. White sacrifices a pawn to build a strong centre and to open lines for an immediate attack against the enemy king. No more boring Berlins - take the fight to your opponent from the off. This DVD contains all you need to know to tackle your opponent. If you are playing a World Championship match, Daniel King wouldn't recommend playing the King's Gambit. But if that doesn't apply to you, then get stuck in. You have nothing to lose but your bishop's pawn!

29,90 €

ChessBase GmbH · News: en.chessbase.com · CB Shop: shop.chessbase.com
CHESSBASE DEALER: NEW IN CHESS · P.O. Box 1093 · NL-1810 KB Alkmaar
phone (+31)72 5127137 · fax (+31)72 5158234 · WWW.NEWINCHESS.COM

An unforgettable interview that never took place

Perfume for Klara Shagenovna

'I paid my bill, and, to my surprise, was given an envelope with a small photo of the interview session, without any further text. The receptionist shrugged his shoulders. Someone had delivered it in the morning.'

In 1984, he wasn't World Champion yet, but all the experts agreed that Gari (not yet Garry) Kasparov would soon claim the highest title. Equally convinced, the newly established magazine New In Chess sent off **ALEXANDER MÜNNINGHOFF** to Baku to interview the phenomenon. As a tribute to a great friend and writer, who sadly died on April 28, we bring you his account of this memorable trip that he wrote in 2007 for the Dutch literary chess magazine *Matten*.

'Are you coming all the way from the Netherlands to Baku to interview me? Cool!'

It was early 1984, and Gari Kasparov (20), who had just qualified for the semi-final of the Candidates Matches, where he would face old Vasily Smyslov in the Lithuanian city of Vilnius, was clearly not yet a spoilt prima donna, let alone the ruthless chess despot or the passionate political Don Quixote we would come to know later. On the creaky telephone line that connected The Hague with the Soviet outlying district of Azerbaijan, after countless interventions via Moscow, the Red Capital, I heard the young, excited voice of someone who was starting to realize what worldwide prospects were offered to him by his enormous talent, and was eager for all the new experiences connected with this.

soon!' he shouted before hanging up. His voice sounded genuinely enthusiastic.

Stopover to meet Botvinnik

Since not only all communication lines went via Moscow in the Union of Soviet Socialist Republics in that time, but also all transit flights (there were neither direct flights from abroad to Baku, nor to any other capital in the republics that had joined the USSR), it seemed a good idea to stop over in Moscow for a day to talk to Mikhail Botvinnik, the ancient patriarch of the Soviet chess world. After all, Botvinnik had had both Karpov, who was World Champion at the time, and the upcoming talent Kasparov as his pupils. And since I had built up an excellent relationship with Mikhail Moiseevich over the years (I always regarded him as a model of the sincere, principled, and therefore

I heard the young, excited voice of someone who was starting to realize what worldwide prospects were offered to him by his enormous talent

One of which, as said, was an interview with a Dutch journalist who, for the sake of exclusiveness, was sent to the Caucasian metropolis Baku, Kasparov's birthplace and place of residence, by the publisher of the recently established magazine New In Chess. Wim Andriessen also expected me, apart from coming up with a good story, to come to a reasonable agreement on the fee Kasparov would receive for his analysis of a few recent games.

On the telephone we noted down a few periods during which Kasparov would certainly be in Baku, and would be able to talk to me. We agreed that I would call him as soon as I arrived. 'Fine, great! See you

respectable Communist), I assumed that he would be forthcoming with information that I would be able to use for the interview with Kasparov.

I wasn't wrong about that. Botvinnik welcomed me punctually at the agreed hour, in the House of Friendship with Peoples of Foreign Countries on what was then still called Kalinin Prospekt in Moscow. While we drank tea, Botvinnik told me about the substantial differences between his two star pupils: 'Karpov is a practical player, Kasparov is a researcher. The practical player puts his trust in his talent when he's sitting at the board, and that's how it is with Tolya: even in his sleep, in a manner of speaking, he puts his knight on

the right square, the one demanded by the position. But Garik examines the game in order to become a better practical player. And while doing this, he also examines himself, with the intention to bring his own qualities to the fore in a game, and to hide his weaknesses. All of this characterizes the researcher. The match between Karpov and Kasparov [Botvinnik had already indicated that, despite his appreciation for Smyslov, he believed that Kasparov would eventually be the one playing for the title – A.M.] will, for this reason, become the third top duel of this century. The first was Capablanca versus Alekhine in 1927. Capablanca was a fabulous talent, but he studied little. Alekhine, on the other hand, was a good researcher. Then the second top match was the one between Tal and me in 1960. Again, the same motif, and we will certainly see this return in Karpov-Kasparov.'

Of course, I was silently surprised that Botvinnik had not included Spassky-Fischer in this short list – the clash that we Western sensation-seekers had long since elevated to the status of Match of the Century. Apparently, the legendary former World Champion considered the criterion of pragmatist versus theoretician to be the dominating factor, and that was something he hadn't detected in the Reykjavik 1972 match. Was he right? I was searching for an answer to this question. By 1984, Boris Vasilievich's laziness after his defeat in 1972 had already become so proverbial that he surely had to be placed in the camp of practical players. Just like Capablanca in his day, Spassky sometimes appeared at the board in tennis clothes, and personally, as his daily sparring partner on the court during an IBM tournament in Amsterdam, I had even seen him arrive late in the tournament hall for this reason.

But then, couldn't Fischer lay claim to being a researcher? Perhaps not, if we look more closely.

Leiden 1970. Mikhail Botvinnik talks while Boris Spassky, Bent Larsen (who had a reasonable command of the Russian language) and Alexander Münninghoff (the interpreter for the Russian participants) express reservation and amusement.

I remembered that precisely in that one game against Botvinnik, the only game ever between the two, at the Varna Olympiad in 1962, the great researcher had prepared an opening variation in the Grünfeld at home, and Fischer refuted the line *over the board* with a pseudo-sacrifice of the queen. The fact that the game was narrowly held to a draw despite an extra pawn for the American was due to a number of human factors: firstly, Botvinnik was peeved that he hadn't done his homework well, and missed a couple of good continuations that seemed to guarantee a draw. Secondly, Fischer started to act in a theatrically boorish manner, and, consequently, started playing carelessly because he thought that Botvinnik was playing on for too long in a lost position. And eventually, Botvinnik's teammate Geller managed, after a lengthy nocturnal analysis, to find the saving drawing line which Botvinnik reproduced flawlessly the next day. Fischer had been comfortably sleeping that night, convinced of his coming win. No – in the eyes of the dedicated Soviet chess player Botvinnik, the fickle, morally unstable, over-confident Fischer

simply could not claim to have played a Match of the Century.

But apparently, Karpov and Kasparov could. This was going to be a clash between two styles – or attitudes to life, if one prefers. Much more interesting, Botvinnik opined, than the superficial Cold War squabbles with Spassky and Fischer. For a moment, I thought about the bone-lazy Karpov, who liked to stay in bed until the afternoon, and in his ample free time could often be seen standing at the pinball machine or the billiards table, and compared him with the zealous Kasparov who, in this pre-computer age, covered entire school notebooks with scribblings of brand-new razor-sharp variations he had invented himself, and who trained physically till he dropped on the beach of the Caspian Sea. I was barely able to suppress a certain preference for Karpov.

It was actually curious, so it occurred to me, that within a totalitarian system two so diametrically opposed lifestyles could exist side by side at the highest level in such an important branch of sports – or rather: that both styles were accepted by the Party. Once I found myself on this track, I immediately realized something I had, of course, already known for a long time: in the USSR, anyone who showed appealing results in the international arena could permit himself anything – which was the case with Karpov. If you hadn't come that far yet, you still had to work hard for some time – like Kasparov.

Heydar Aliyev

There were more things going on in the background. Not long before this time, in late 1982, Heydar Aliyev, the leader of the Azerbaijan Communist Party, had been promoted by the new party leader in Moscow, Leonid Brezhnev's successor Yury Andropov, to full member of the almighty Politburo. Aliyev was the first Turkish-speaking member of this board. He had already been enrolled as a candidate member under Brezhnev. Everyone knew that Brezhnev had pushed Karpov enormously, and had showered the frail youngster from Zlatust with favours and decorations after the latter had beaten the depraved renegade Viktor Kortchnoi in the Philippines. Of course, within the broader Soviet context, and following in Brezhnev's tracks, Aliyev also showed adherence to Karpov. But when it turned out that with Kasparov he had a future World Champion within the walls of his own city Baku, he didn't hesitate to support this new star in every possible way. In the extremely complicated power struggle within the USSR in those days, in which any positioning in the Kremlin was closely connected to successes and triumphs accomplished by one's own supporters, this had been an understandable move by Aliyev. After all, it was better to have a strong trump up your sleeve, just in case. As far as my information reached, it had been especially Kasparov's mother, Klara Shagenovna, who had drawn Aliyev's attention to her son's prospects.

I thought this was an intriguing piece of information which had to be studied in more depth. What did this support by Aliyev involve exactly? What did he want in return? Had this *démarche* by the mother been absolutely necessary? Would Kasparov never have been able to emerge as a top player without that support? How much Azeri nationalism was behind this? I could answer this latter question straightaway, since Klara was an Armenian, and father Weinstein was a Jew. Didn't that place Kasparov outside of society in Baku? But 'Communist nationalism', in the sense that within the community of the USSR in Moscow, advantages for the Azerbaijan Soviet Socialist Republic could be obtained with the help of high achievers like Kasparov – that was something I could imagine. I realized that this was a very delicate subject, but I was determined to try and find out about this via all kinds of roundabout routes.

When we parted, Botvinnik, as if he could read my mind, asked if I had already met Klara Shagenovna. 'I haven't met her, but I've heard a lot about her', I replied, and immediately asked what he thought of her. 'Unmistakably, she has a good influence on her son', Botvinnik said. 'She protects him from the outside world, takes the first blows, and preserves him from unpleasant things.' I said that I had brought a set of perfume bottles for her. 'O, *Vy svetski tsjelovjek, Aleksandr Fyodorovich*', Botvinnik said smilingly, patting me on the back. 'You are a man of the world.'

Downright inquisitive

The next evening, after a flight of over three hours from Moscow to Baku, I immediately phoned Gari from my hotel room. But the telephone was answered by Shagenovna. 'Where are you?' she asked, and after I had said 'Gostinitsa Sovjetskaja' she continued without further ado, 'I'm coming to see you. I'll be there in half an hour.'

This was an energetic approach I hadn't reckoned with. Within two months, Gari would be 21, an adult man according to the law, but apparently other rules prevailed at the Kasparov home. I hadn't even got him on the phone! For a while, I considered calling again, using the fact that she was on her way to me, but I thought this might be just a little too provocative. So, meekly, I took the present I had brought out of my suitcase and waited for the phone call from reception that would announce the arrival of *madame* in a chair at the window, where a dreary, untidy

'Please sit down', she ordered, as if she had taken over my room and the only thing she had to do was discuss a few formalities

lace curtain obstructed the view of a badly-lit, virtually deserted square.

Wrong again. Suddenly I heard a fierce knock on the door. I opened it, and before I even had a chance to introduce myself, a resolute figure made its way past me. 'Please sit down', she ordered, as if she had taken over my room and the only thing she had to do was discuss a few formalities. She had already taken a seat herself.

From the very start, the atmosphere between us was uncomfortable, and, on her part, downright inquisitive. When I trotted out the tax-free perfume set from Schiphol Airport, she put it aside with a resolute gesture and inquired: 'What are you planning to ask to my son?'

There I was – a man of the world. I had to think of this story by Euwe. When he played Vera Menchik for the first time, he brought her a bunch of flowers. Doubtlessly with a gesture just as emphatic as Klara Shagenovna's, Miss Menchik removed it from

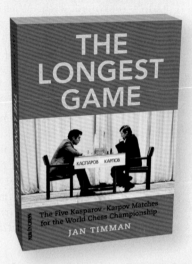
the playing table. Women who come for business are essentially monomaniacal, and only throw their femininity into the fray when they have learned to do so.

Klara Shagenovna was in the first instance a Soviet mother, and hadn't mastered this subtlety (yet). With her dark eyes, painted lips and reddish-brown hairdo, she made a militant impression. It was easily imaginable that she could be very charming, but in this conversation her behaviour was characterized by deep suspicion against me and the entire evil, unreliable Western world that I represented in her eyes. Her whole being radiated only one deep wish: to protect her son Gari from the outside world, and preserve him against unpleasant things. Exactly as Botvinnik had said. Only, at that point he had gathered almost half a century of practical experience with the West, and, knowing that it wouldn't be that bad, he spoke from a tower of calm unassailability. Klara Shagenovna stood at the beginning of the career of her son, for whom she had given up her job at the electro-technical laboratory of the Azerbaijan Academy of Science a few months earlier. Without any doubt, she was still caught up in the totalitarian system that would have to facilitate Garik's meteoric rise. That, and nothing else, was her beacon. I was disturbing the clucky hen's rest. She was extremely on her guard, ready to shoot me down at the slightest sign of danger. I understood that.

But at the same time, I had this problem. New In Chess, that had started so ambitiously, would not be amused if after such an expensive trip I came back without the hoped-for interview for the first issue of the magazine!

In a desperate effort, I started going through my list of questions with her. The first series concerned Garik's background: family, father died young, school, first steps in the chess world. Klara Shagenovna gave no noticeable reaction, nor did she when I recited the second series to her. These were technical questions about his method of preparation, his research of openings, his time as a pupil of Botvinnik, and his assessment of his future opponents. She listened attentively, her features seemed to soften a little, and when the first approving nod came, the ice seemed, if not to break, then at least to melt a little.

But when she listened to the next series of questions, which could be summarized under the heading 'Current Situation and Prospects for the Future', she was suddenly at war again. 'You will not ask that question,' she hissed after I had mentioned the possible role of Heydar Aliyev in the developing process of her son, stashed away in a mumbled subordinate clause. Her eyes flashed with anger, and her red fingernails clasped her handbag like a tiger's claws. She gazed hard at me, and repeated, 'You will not ask that question. Under no condition.'

I don't recall how long I've been trying to talk Klara Shagenovna round after this. Probably not more than ten minutes, but it seemed to take an hour before she complied to my proposal of a compromise. The interview would take place on the next day, at two o'clock in the afternoon, in the house of the Sports Committee of the Azerbaijan Soviet Socialist Republic. Gari would bring his own tape recorder and record the conversation, so that his mother could listen to it at home. Should it happen that she heard something she didn't like, then we would talk about it, and then, if she insisted, I wouldn't use it in my story. I gave her my word of honour, and assured her that I would do everything to treat this operation '*po dzjentlmenski*'.

With that, our conversation was concluded. Klara Shagenovna left without any noticeable greeting. After some insistence from my side, she eventually did take the perfume with her. This felt like a small, unex-

pected victory on a strange and shadowy battlefield, the contours of which I could not sharply visualize; but it seemed that there wasn't much good in store for me.

Eavesdroppers

This feeling worsened when, the next morning, I got a phone call from a local journalist from, if I remember rightly, the *Bakinski Rabotsji* ('The Baku Worker'). I don't remember his name, but I do recall that I suddenly became aware that my interview with Gari Kasparov was clearly no longer a personal tête-à-tête with, at most, his mother present in the background. The entire project had been embedded in a much larger one, in which many people unknown to me were in the know – perhaps even involved. And on account of the weight attached to Gari Kasparov, there was now probably a small file on the project on some desk somewhere in the highest echelons of the Communist Party. This 'colleague', as he introduced himself, asked if I had any objections to him attending the

My interview with Gari Kasparov was clearly no longer a personal tête-à-tête

interview. After all, Gari didn't give so many interviews, he said. And, if it was allowed, he would also bring a photographer. I replied that this was fine with me. In the meantime, I tried to imagine what the situation would be like at the Kasparov home. It seemed clear to me that with this journalist, Klara had called in reinforcements to be present during the conversation as eavesdroppers, and would report any possible *faux pas* to her, or to God knows whom from the Central Committee if necessary. Also, I had no doubt that she had urged her son to avoid politically-tinted questions, and to install and use his tape recorder properly. All this was, of course, very double. Apparently, nothing must be allowed to go wrong. But my Western

mind shouldn't worry too much about that, I told myself. The main thing was that the interview for New In Chess would take place.

At half past one, as agreed, two gentlemen were standing in the hotel lobby, waiting for me: the colleague and the photographer. Since it was my first time in Baku, I asked if they could accompany me to the house of the Sports Committee. It turned out to be nearby. We went there on foot. The conversation along the way was very Soviet: the colleague was specialized in several sports, so he told me, and on that account he had been abroad more than once – yes, even to the West. He summed up: *Frantsija, Velikobritanija, Belgija, Finlandija.* The photographer, who hadn't been anywhere, trudged along with us dejectedly, conscious of the fact that this unasked-for litany was mainly intended to emphasize the hierarchy between him and his colleague. I kept silent for most of the time, concen-

trating on the approaching conversation with Kasparov.

Sports Committee

The house of the Sports Committee was one of those typical dismal Soviet bunkers that you can still come across everywhere in the Russian Federation. A facade and a landing that did not exactly invite one in – on the contrary, you somehow got the feeling that you weren't at all welcome. This feeling was intensified by the desk at the entrance with the ubiquitous militia men asking you icily for your '*dokoementy*', studying your passport carefully, and then calling the department in question deep inside the building with a telephone made of childish yellow rinky-dink plastic. That's how it was here, too. After some time, a nondescript young man turned up. He led us to a small conference room without saying a word. Without any further explanation, the man left again, closing the door behind him.

I decided to install myself, preparing my writing pad, pen and tape recorder, and conversing with the photographer, who was laboriously unpacking screens and mirrors that he thought were necessary to do his job properly. The colleague had found a spot next to me.

After a few minutes, the door burst open, and there he was: Gari Kasparov. Smiling, and with his hand outstretched, he walked up to me.

I have to say that he made a very convincing impression on me. With his dynamic way of speaking and moving, and his modern clothes (he was wearing a fashionable jacket and a ditto shirt of Western tailoring), he was every inch a representative of the new Soviet chess generation who were about to make it to the top. When we made our acquaintance, he asked politely whether my long journey had gone well, showed interest in my meeting with Botvinnik, indicated briefly that we also had some business to discuss, and finally declared himself ready to answer all my questions. While he made this last announcement, he put his own tape recorder on the table with a snigger – not mentioning his mother.

Gari, the colleague and I pressed the buttons of our recording devices all at approximately the same time, the photographer focussed his lenses, and I asked my first question. Things went entirely according to the scenario I had gone through with Klara Shagenovna: tell me something about your youth.

Kasparov was busy giving an answer for one-and-a-half, maybe two minutes. The sun shone through the window, the photograph was fiddling a little with his screens and mirrors, and snapped. I smiled encouragingly to Garik. The interview was starting to get going, it was looking good. He looked back with a friendly expression.

A few seconds later, suddenly, without knocking, the door of the room was opened and a small man in a black leather jacket appeared on the doorstep. Without introducing himself, he addressed Kasparov directly with the words: 'Gari, you have to come to the Sports

Alexander Münninghoff catches up with Boris Spassky during the 1978 Interpolis tournament in Tilburg.

Committee right away. Unfortunately the interview has to be terminated.' After these words, he kept waiting on the doorstep.

While I looked around flabbergasted, searching for help and support, Kasparov jumped up. 'Well dammit, now that's annoying', he said, and, turning to the man in the doorpost: 'How long will this take? Can our guest wait until I'm ready?' The man shook his head silently. 'Well,' Kasparov said, 'then there's nothing for it but to make a new appointment. You understand, the Sports Committee... If you can call me tonight around nine, then we will fix this. Sorry that it had to turn out this way, but there's nothing I can do. Goodbye.' And then he was gone.

'Gee,' the colleague said, taken aback, 'I've never seen anything like this.' We looked at each other, shrugged our shoulders, and went on our way back to the hotel. The photographer took his leave along the way; he promised to give me a print of that one photo he had been able to make. I agreed with the colleague

that he would call me later that evening, around ten, when I would inform him about the new appointment. 'Do you think it is still going to happen?' I asked, in a sudden impulse. He looked at me doubtfully. Then he said, *'Jesjo nje vetsjer.* The day isn't over yet, things can still take a favourable turn.' As it turned out, these were the last words I heard from this confrere.

Reporting trip to Tbilisi

That evening, at nine o'clock, I got Klara Shagenovna on the line again – I had been expecting this. 'Gari is asleep now, and I'm going to let him sleep,' she said, 'he is dead tired. That meeting with the Sports Committee took hours.' On my question whether a new arrangement for the interview had been made, she replied coolly: 'That is something Gari has to arrange with you himself, that's not my business.' I agreed with her that I would call the next morning at ten o'clock.

One hour later I realized that things were quite amiss. My fellow journalist didn't call and didn't call, and finally I tried his home number. A stressed woman's voice told me that her husband had suddenly left for a three-day reporting trip to Tbilisi in Georgia.

Sitting in my gloomy Hotel Sovjetskaja room, I took stock. Of course, that colleague had been informed in the meantime that the interview was called off, and he had made up this idiotic excuse so that he didn't have to look me in the face again. Who had told him that the deal was off was unclear, however. Klara Shagenovna? That would mean that she had disregarded my word of honour, which was a thoughtlessness that was quite unimaginable in the Caucasus. No, it was much more likely that the party officials were behind this. After all, they didn't have anything to do with me – as witness the complete non-communication between me and the man who came to collect Kasparov during the interview. They had decided to fob me off, and there was nothing I could do about it. Still,

Walk in the park

The next morning at ten o'clock I got Kasparov himself on the line for the first time. I had expected this, since after all we still had to talk business about the fee for the analyses, and I had gathered that such talks enjoyed a certain priority with him. In fact, this was my last hope of getting something like an interview, and so I jumped to my feet when he proposed to meet me in the small park in front of the hotel at twelve o'clock sharp to discuss these financial details.

The reader should keep in mind that in 1984, the USSR was a country where foreigners were kept under close surveillance. It was also standard procedure to tap phone conversations, certainly with a journalist who was regarded as unwelcome by the Party. I realized that by now I had come to belong to that category: not only had I got that midnight phone call, but in the morning, right after my conversation with Gari, I got an unknown man on

to twelve. With an uncanny feeling I went outside and walked into the small park.

The following scene may appear incredible to the Western reader, but sure enough, at the stroke of twelve there was some rustling in the bushes, and out came Gari Kasparov! 'Follow me', he spoke in an imperative tone, walking away quickly – I could hardly keep up with him. I knew that Fischer was reputed to be a kind of heel-and-toe walker, but this really took the cake. We turned one corner, then another one a little further on, and then found ourselves in a crowded shopping street. There, Gari slowed down a little, and looked at me expectantly. 'Well?' he said.

I reacted grudgingly at first: 'What about our interview? We agreed on that, didn't we? Do you realize I've come all the way from the Netherlands? And what do you mean by "Well?!", feigning ignorance. He grinned apologetically, saying there was nothing he could do about it, and pointed vaguely around him, announcing: 'The walls have ears here, please understand me.'

Suddenly I'd had more than enough of it. The eternal twisting and scheming in this country! 'I offer you eight hundred dollars for three game analyses,' I said. Kasparov looked around for a moment, apparently to find a spot where the walls didn't have ears, and then whispered: 'Eight hundred, that's a number with two zeros. I was thinking of a number with three zeros.'

I told him I would pass on the message, and that I thought it was an utter disgrace that the interview had fallen through. He spread his arms in a powerless gesture, turned around, and disappeared into the crowd.

'Nothing beats returning home having achieved nothing', Ton Sijbrands (Dutch former draughts World Champion – ed.) used to say. A resigned sigh that had found its way into my vocabulary, but that offered precious little solace this time. ∎

Kasparov whispered: 'Eight hundred, that's a number with two zeros. I was thinking of a number with three zeros.'

it was Gari Kasparov's attitude that interested me most. He had looked so genuinely surprised when our conversation was broken off, and his promise to make a new appointment had sounded credible. Had it all been nothing but show? Or was Gari also directed by the officials? Whatever the case – the next night I had a flight back to Moscow, so I could forget about that interview for New In Chess. As if to confirm this cheerless understanding, I got a phone call from an unknown man around midnight, who advised me not to stick my nose into other people's business. When I asked angrily what he meant, the man hung up.

the line who asked me if I wanted to exchange currency. This time, I hung up immediately – any word against this provocateur would have been one too many and, therefore, dangerous.

I decided to check out first. In the lobby, I seemed to notice that there were more security people walking around than in the previous two days. I paid my bill, and, to my surprise, was given an envelope with a small photo of the interview session, without any further text. The receptionist shrugged his shoulders. Someone had delivered it in the morning. I put the envelope in my suitcase and took the suitcase to the luggage room. It was two minutes

WINNER

Chess.com

TEAM **CHINA**

WEI YI / DING LIREN / WANG HAO / HOU YIFAN / YU YANGYI / JU WENJUN

Captain: Ye Jiangchuan

#NationsCup

The line-up of the winning Chinese team: Wei Yi, Ding Liren, Wang Hao, Hou Yifan, Yu Yangyi and Ju Wenjun.

China prevails in Nations Cup

Yu Yangyi in great shape

Hot on the heels of the Magnus Carlsen Invitational, FIDE and Chess.com organized another top-level online event, the Nations Cup. **JAN TIMMAN** watched a close race, decided by a disputable tiebreak rule that gave China drawing odds in the final against the USA.

It's been a novel experience the past weeks. When you download the latest harvest of games from TWIC, you see just a few hundred games on your screen instead of the plentiful harvest of thousands that we were used to. And not a single classical game amongst

them. These are hard times for the true chess addict. The online game lacks that thrill and tension; for that, you need to be at a board, not in front of a screen. I myself do not suffer: I can satisfy my craving by writing books, analysing games and composing endgame studies. I have never ventured into online

playing. I don't see the attraction.

In the absence of classical tournaments, people hastily organized several online events. The day after the Magnus Carlsen Invitational on Chess24 saw the start of the Online Nations Cup, a FIDE initiative in collaboration with Chess.com. It didn't qualify as a replacement for the postponed Olympiad, of course, but it wasn't a bad idea: six four-player teams meeting in a double-round competition, with the two top finishers battling for the honours in a separate final. The make-up of the teams was necessarily somewhat arbitrary. Besides four strong chess countries – China, India, Russia

Nothing much is happening. At best, White may be slightly better because his king is safer, but a draw seems the most likely outcome.

46.♕e7 ♗c2?

Black had already switched his bishop between b3 and c2 a few times, but this time it's a decisive error. With 46...♕g5+ Black could have ensured a

48...h5 49.g5 h4 50.a4

The a-pawn has been unleashed. Black is powerless.

50...♔g8 51.a5 ♔h7 52.a6 ♗d1 53.♔xd1 d2 54.♕xg7+ ♔xg7 55.♗xg7 ♔xg7 56.♔xd2

Black resigned.

Instructive mistakes

I have always found it hard to commentate rapid games, but in some cases a game is instructive precisely because of the mistakes it contains. An example is the following duel, from the match Europe-India, every stage of which is full of tension.

The online game lacks that thrill and tension; for that, you need to be at a board

and the US – there were teams from 'Europe' and 'The Rest of the World'. With the exception of the World Champion, virtually all top players participated. For added lustre, two former World Champions acted as team captains – Kasparov for Europe and Kramnik for India.

The time-control was 25 minutes with 10-second increments, which meant that the players had 10 minutes more per game than in the Magnus Carlsen Invitational. I have the feeling that this raised the level of play a little bit, although this would be hard to ascertain. However this may be, I was pleasantly surprised when I saw the following fragment from the Round 3 match between Europe and India.

Levon Aronian
Vidit Gujrathi
Nations Cup 2020 (3)

position after 45...♗b3

theoretically drawn endgame; he could also have put his bishop somewhere on the a2-g8 diagonal.

47.b4!! A fantastic move.
47...axb3 48.♗b2!

The point of the pawn sacrifice: the black bishop is side-lined completely, and the advanced passed pawns are in the way. In the previous issue, I alluded to the connection between the endgame study and the practical game. Aronian gave me a tailor-made example: what we see here is an undiluted study motif.

Jan-Krzysztof Duda
Pentala Harikrishna
Nations Cup 2020 (8)
Queen's Gambit, Alatortsev Variation

1.d4 d5 2.c4 e6 3.♘c3 ♗e7 4.cxd5 exd5 5.♗f4 c6 6.e3 ♗f5 7.♘ge2 ♘d7 8.♘g3 ♗g6 9.h4

A speculative pawn sacrifice that has rarely been played.

9...h5

Now White's approach has been justified. Black should have accepted the sacrifice. 9...♗xh4 10.♘h5 ♔f8 11.♕b3 leads to a sharp position with chances for both sides.

10.♗d3 ♗xd3 11.♕xd3 g6 12.e4 ♘gf6

He should in any case have tried 12...♘b6.

13.e5 ♘h7

A passive square for the knight, but after 13...♘g4 White would cut off the knight's retreat with 14.♕d2, with a large advantage.

14.e6

Obvious and strong. The black king is forced to an unsafe part of the board.

14...♘df8 15.exf7+ ♔xf7 16.♗e5 White has won the opening. Now he must break through the black defences.

16...♖g8 17.f4 Far stronger was 17.0-0-0, intending to meet 17...♗xh4 calmly with 18.♔b1. Advancing the f-pawn is not a priority, since Black has no counterplay.

17...♗xh4

18.f5 White's best bet was still castling queenside. After the hasty text Black grabs the initiative.

18...♗xg3+ 19.♗xg3

19...♕g5! A powerful move. Black prevents queenside castling and will use the half-open g-file to launch an attack once White has castled kingside.

20.0-0 ♘f6 21.♗f4 ♕g4 22.♘d1 ♖e8 23.♘e3

23...♖xe3!

A strong exchange sacrifice cementing Black's initiative.

24.♗xe3 gxf5 25.♕c2

25...♘e6

Very strong was 25...♔e6!, a king move à la Petrosian. The king is safe in the middle, because Black has square e4 for his knight. A possible continuation is 26.♖f4 ♕h3 27.♕e2 ♘e4 28.♖e1 ♖g3, with a strong initiative.

26.♖xf5 ♘xd4 27.♗xd4 ♕xd4+ 28.♕f2 ♕xf2+ 29.♖xf2 ♔e6

In this endgame, the chances are roughly equal.

30.♖af1 ♖g6 31.♖e1+ ♔d6 32.♖f5 d4 33.♖a5

A rather pointless manoeuvre. 33.♔f2 would have balanced the position.

33...a6 34.♖d1 ♖g4 35.♖f5 ♔e6 36.♖df1 ♖g6 37.♖5f4 ♔e5 38.♖f5+ ♔e6 39.♖5f4 ♔e5

40.a4 Is Duda playing for a win? If so, that would be a risky idea, since he had two minutes against Harikrishna's four.

40...♘d5 41.♖f5+ ♔e4 42.♖xh5 ♘e3

White has won a pawn, but his passed g-pawn is harmless and the black knight is very strong. Black is better.

43.♖f2

43...d3

An instructive error. Black should have kept the knight's strong foothold and penetrated with his king with 43...♔d3. After the text the position is equal again.

44.♖h4+ ♖g4 45.♖h7 b5 46.♖h6 ♘c4 47.♖xc6 ♔e3

Stronger was 47...♖g5, trying to get the rook behind the passed pawn.

48.axb5 axb5 49.♖e6+ ♚d4 50.♖e8

In Round 5, India took an early lead against Russia when Ian Nepomniachtchi played a move that, as his opponent Vishy Anand knew, led to a forced loss.

50...d2

Now the proud pawn will be lost. With 50...b4 Black could have kept it.

51.♖d8+ ♚c5 52.b3 ♘a5 53.♖f3 ♖b4 54.♖xd2 ♘xb3 55.♖c2+ ♖c4 56.♖f5+ ♚d6 57.♖a2 ♘d4 58.♖a6+ ♖c6 59.♖f6+ ♚d5 60.♖fxc6 ♘xc6

61.♖b6

61.♚f2 would have won more quickly. According to the Tablebases it's mate in 33.

61...♚c5 62.♖b7 b4 63.♚f2 ♘a5 64.♖b8 ♘c6 65.♖b7 ♘a5 66.♖a7

The correct way was 66.♖c7+, with mate in 41.

66...♘c6 After 66...♘c4 White would have had a practical problem. The only winning move is 67.♖b7, but that would have led to three times the same position.

67.♖a1 Now the rest is simple.

67...b3 68.♖c1+ ♚b5 69.♚e3 ♘e7 70.♚d2 ♘d5 71.♖c8 ♘f4 72.g4 ♘e6 73.♚c3 ♘c5 74.♚b2 ♚b4 75.g5 ♘d3+ 76.♚b1 ♘e5 77.♖e8 ♘f3 78.g6

Black resigned.

Anand's deja vu

It was good to see Anand active again. He was playing from Germany, where he was stranded by the lock-down. Against Nepomniachtchi he showed his famously deep preparation.

**Vishy Anand
Ian Nepomniachtchi**
Nations Cup 2020 (5)
Grünfeld Indian, Exchange Variation

1.d4 ♘f6 2.c4 g6 3.♘c3 d5 4.cxd5 ♘xd5 5.♗d2 ♗g7 6.e4 ♘xc3 7.♗xc3 c5 8.d5 ♗xc3+ 9.bxc3 ♕d6 10.♕d2 0-0 11.f4 e6 12.♘f3

In Giri-Vachier-Lagrave in Yekaterinburg, White played 12.♗c4, after which Black countered with 12...b5.

12...exd5 13.♗c4

13...♗e6?

It sounds incredible, but this is already the decisive mistake. And Anand knew it. Better was 13...♘c6, postponing 14...♗e6 till after 14.♗xd5. And if Black wanted to play 13...d4, this was the right moment.

14.0-0 d4

Strangely enough, the situation is hopeless. After 14...♖d8 White would break through with 15.f5, too. After 15...dxc4 16.♕h6 Black has no more defence. The main line goes as follows: 16...♕f8 17.♕h4 gxf5

18.♘g5 h6 19.exf5 ♗d5 20.♘e6!, with annihilation.

15.f5 ♗xc4 16.e5

It's almost impossible to have it easier.

16...♕d7 17.f6 Black resigned.

Yekaterinburg revisited

Online playing doesn't seem to suit Nepomniachtchi. In the Nations Cup he also went under against his great competitor from Yekaterinburg, although it must be said that he did get chances.

Ian Nepomniachtchi
Maxime Vachier-Lagrave
Nations Cup 2020 (6)
Caro-Kann Defence, Advance Variation

1.e4 c6 2.d4 d5 3.e5 ♗f5 4.♘f3 e6 5.♗e2 c5 6.♗e3 ♕b6 7.♘c3 ♘c6 8.♘a4 ♕a5+ 9.c3

9...cxd4

The alternative is 9...c4. In Durarbayli-Suleymanli, Moscow 2020, the play continued 10.♘h4 b5 11.♘xf5 exf5 12.♘c5 ♗xc5 13.dxc5 ♘ge7, with roughly equal chances.

10.♘xd4 ♘xd4 11.♗xd4 ♘e7
12.g4 A sharp move. Most players castle here.

12...♗g6 13.♘c5 ♕c7

14.h4

The alternative 14.f4 would also lead to very sharp play. A possible continuation is 14...♘c6 15.♖f1 h6 16.f5 exf5 17.gxf5 ♗h7, with roughly

Online playing doesn't seem to suit Ian Nepomniachtchi

equal chances. Things are looking a bit scary for Black, but once he has castled queenside, he will automatically get counterplay.

14...h5 15.gxh5 ♗f5 16.♕b3 0-0-0 17.a4

But White must continue to play sharp chess on both wings.

17...♘c6 18.a5

18...♘xd4 The alternative 18...♗xc5

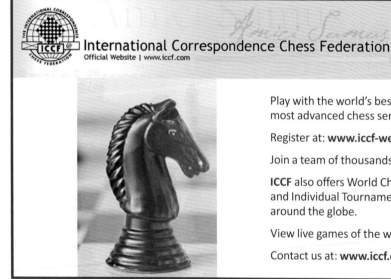

was probably stronger. After 19.♗xc5 ♕xe5 20.a6 b6 21.♗e3 ♕c7 Black has a comfortable position.

19.cxd4 ♗xc5 20.dxc5 ♕xc5

21.0-0

Late castling. White gets just enough compensation for his bad kingside structure.

21...♔b8 22.♖fc1 ♕e7 23.a6 b6 24.♖c6 ♗e4 25.f3

It wasn't his day. Immediately after his loss to Anand, 'Nepo' fought a long battle with Maxime Vachier-Lagrave that ended in another loss after 111 moves.

25...♖xh5!?

Black could also have withdrawn his bishop, with roughly equal chances. But the piece sac is more interesting, and it is justified by practical considerations.

26.fxe4 ♖xh4

A strange position. Which king is less safe? The position is dynamically balanced.

27.♗f3 ♖h3

This provocative move leads to a winning position for Black in the end, but it is not objectively correct.

Stronger was 27...♕g5+, making the draw inevitable. An attractive line is 28.♔f1 ♕f4 29.♖xb6+ ♔a8 30.♖d6 ♖b8 31.♖d8 ♖h1+ 32.♔e2 ♖h2+, with perpetual check.

28.exd5?

Nepomniachtchi had four minutes left here. If he had kept his cool, he would undoubtedly have found the winning 28.♔f1!. Black cannot capture on e4, because he would be mated. The only move is 28...d4, but then White consolidates his position with 29.♖d1. White is winning, because the black attack has stalled.

28...♕g5+ 29.♔f1 ♕f4!

What a change in circumstances. Now Black has a winning attack.

30.♖a3

Sad necessity. After 30.♖xb6+ ♔a8 it would have been curtains for White.

30...♖h1+ 31.♔e2 ♖h2+ 32.♔f1 ♖h1+ 33.♔e2 ♕xe5+ 34.♔d3 ♖xd5+ 35.♗xd5 ♖h3+ 36.♔c2 ♖xb3 37.♖xb3 ♕e2+ 38.♔b1 exd5 39.♖a3 d4 40.♖c2 ♕b5 41.♖d2 ♕f1+ 42.♔a2 ♕c4+ 43.♔b1 g5 44.♖f3

44...g4 A lapse of concentration. 44...♕d5 would have won easily, e.g. 45.♖fd3 ♕e4 46.♔c1 ♕c6+ 47.♔b1 ♕g6, and the connected passed pawn will decide.

45.♖f4 Now two proud passed pawns are lost.

45...g3 46.♖dxd4 ♕e6 47.♖g4 b5 48.♖g8+ ♔c7 49.♖dg4 More accurate was 49.♖d3, after which Black hardly has any winning chances. White missed some more chances to hold and in the end Black won (0-1, 111).

Attractive play

It is always a pleasure to follow Firouzja's games. In the final round, in the match Rest of the World-Russia, he won a strategically strong game against Karjakin.

Sergey Karjakin
Alireza Firouzja
Nations Cup 2020 (9)
Caro-Kann Defence, Advance Variation

1.e4 c6 2.d4 d5 3.e5 ♗f5 4.♘f3 e6 5.♗e2 ♘e7 6.♘bd2 c5 7.dxc5 ♘ec6 8.♘b3

8...♗g4!

Magnus Carlsen did not play in the Nations Cup, but Jan Gustafsson was not the only one who was delighted when he joined the commentary on Chess24.

This strategically strong move was thought up by the Russian GM Maletin.

9.0-0 Interesting is 9.c4, when the play could continue as follows: 9...dxc4 10.♕xd8+ ♔xd8 11.♗xc4 ♗xf3 12.gxf3 ♘xe5 13.♗e2 ♘bc6, and Black has solved his opening problems.

9...♘d7

10.♘e1 Somewhat passive. In Gabrielian-Matlakov, Yekaterinburg

It is always a pleasure to follow Alireza Firouzja's games

2013, there followed 10.♘fd4 ♗xe2 11.♕xe2 ♘xd4 12.♘xd4 ♗xc5 13.c3, with roughly equal chances.

10...♗xe2 11.♕xe2 ♘xc5 Black could also have captured the other pawn. After 11...♘cxe5 12.f4 ♘c6 13.♘d3 the position is equal.

12.♘xc5 ♗xc5 13.♘d3 ♗e7 14.♕g4 ♔f8

15.♕h5 A waste of time. Correct was 15.c3.

15...♔g8 16.♗e3 ♖c8 17.♖ad1 The classical question: which rook should White play to the middle? 17.♖fd1 would probably have been better here.

17...♕a5

Now White is forced to weaken his queenside somewhat.

18.a3 ♕a4 19.c3 a5 20.♗g5 h6 21.♗xe7 ♘xe7 22.h3 ♘f5 23.♖fe1 ♖c4

It is clear that Black is calling the shots.

24.g3

An unnecessary weakening. 24.♕f3 looked better.

24...♕c6 25.♕f3 h5 26.♘f4 g6 27.♖d2 b5 28.♘d3 g5

Play on both wings.

29.♕g2 ♔f8 30.♔h2 ♔e7 31.♕h1 ♖d8 32.♖ed1 ♖e4 33.♕g2 ♕c4

Black increases the pressure.

34.♔g1 ♖g8 35.♕h1 ♖g6 36.♕g2

36...♘h4 Objectively speaking, this knight move isn't even all that strong, but it shows clearly how attractive Firouzja's way of playing is.

37.♕h1 g4!? The consequence of the previous move. It has become a real piece sacrifice.

38.gxh4

You can't blame Karjakin for not finding the miraculous rescue move 38.b3!! with only four minutes on the clock. The idea of this pawn move is to force the black queen off the fourth rank. After 38...♕xc3 39.gxh4 gxh3+ 40.♔h2 ♖g2+ 41.♔xh3 ♖gg4 42.♕f3 there's no win for Black.

38...gxh3+ 39.♔f1 h2!

White resigned. If he captures on h2, his queen will be trapped.

China wins again

Although the Russians had fielded a strong team, they played no part in the battle for first place. That was fought between China and the US, with China having the advantage that one of its four boards was occupied by a woman: Hou Yifan was there and she did very well, scoring 4 from 5. The former Women's World Champion annotates her fine win against Mariya Muzychuk ('Rest of the World') in Round 1.

NOTES BY
Hou Yifan

**Mariya Muzychuk
Hou Yifan**
Nations Cup 2020 (1)
Sicilian Defence, Moscow Variation

It was a great pleasure to represent China in the Online Nations Cup in the current global situation. The innovative way of composing the teams, an official online tournament at the highest level, etc., all this made this event super-meaningful.

Personally, I was very happy to join and contribute my efforts to help the team win the tournament, although this was mainly due to the excellent performance of my team mates.

1.e4 c5 2.♘f3 d6 3.♗b5+ ♗d7 4.♗xd7+ ♕xd7 5.c4 e5

One of the latest tries by Carlsen, Caruana and others.

6.♘c3 ♘c6 7.d3 g6

7...♗e7 is another interesting idea,

with the plan ...♗d8, ...♘ge7, followed by ...♗b6 at some moment to free up the bishop.

8.a3 ♗g7 9.b4

9...♘ge7

The pawn is quite poisonous: 9...cxb4? 10.axb4 ♘xb4 11.♗a3 ♘a6 (hoping to block the a3-bishop on c5) 12.♘b5 ♘c5, but now White has 13.♘xe5! ♗xe5 14.d4, and Black's position is too fragile to hold.

10.♖b1 0-0 11.0-0 h6 12.♘d5 f5

Probably a bit premature. More stable was 12...♔h7, protecting both the g6- and the h6-pawn.

13.b5

13...♘d8 Trying to keep the game complex, but this is a bit over-ambitious. The natural reaction was 13...♘d4 14.♘xd4 exd4 15.♘xe7+ ♕xe7 16.exf5 ♖xf5 17.f4, which is slightly worse for Black, as the bishop is of the same colour as the squares of the pawn chain. However, with the flexibility to push ...d5, the position is tenable, albeit with some discomfort.

14.♘h4! Targeting the unprotected g6-pawn. This is the reason why ...♔h7 was recommended earlier.

After her stint as a commentator (together with Peng Zhaoqin) at the Candidates tournament in Yekaterinburg, Hou Yifan was happy to play chess herself again. From home, without a mask.

14...♘xd5

Here I spent quite some time to come to a decision. If 14...♔h7, then 15.exf5! The correct move-order to retain the d5-outpost for the knight. 15...♘xf5 16.♘xf5 gxf5 17.f4 favours White both positionally and dynamically.

15.cxd5 ♔h7 16.exf5 g5

The only move. This was the idea behind exchanging on d5 first. I decided to prioritize the prevention of the f4-break.

17.♘f3

17.f6!? was subtle: 17...♗xf6 18.♘f3 ♘f7 19.♘d2 ♘h8 20.♘e4 ♘g6 21.♕h5 (the kingside is the right area for the queen) 21...♔g7.

17...♕xf5

Suddenly the position has changed, but the evaluation is still in favour of the white side. The doubled d-pawns give White outposts on both e4 and on c4, which restrain the bad bishop on g7.

However, the position is relatively close to equal, since Black is keeping control of the f4-break. In addition, thanks to the b7- and a7-pawns, it is not easy for White to open the queenside either. Therefore, based on the above judgement, I decided to play quietly.

18.♕b3 ♘f7

There is only one road to Rome: ...♘h8-g6!

19.♘d2 ♘h8 20.♘e4

20...♕d7?
Actually, I spent quite some time on the most natural option 20...♖ad8, but 21.♕a4 ♕d7 22.♕xa7 ♖a8 23.♕b6 bothered me and I had missed 23...♖fd8!, after which the white queen is stuck on b6.

21.♗e3 Here White missed a great opportunity to use the e4-knight: 21.♕d1! (stopping ...♘g6) 21...♔g8 (21...♕f7? 22.♗xg5) 22.h4! gxh4 23.♕h5, and White has successfully opened the position.
21...♘g6 22.f3 ♖ad8 23.♕c4 ♔h8 24.a4 ♕f7 25.a5 ♘e7 26.♘c3 ♘f5 27.♗d2 ♘d4 28.♗e3 ♘c2 29.♕e4 29.♗c1 would lead to a repetition. **29...♘xe3 30.♕xe3**

30...e4!?

'When time is running out, people tend to make emotional decisions...'

Objectively, this may not be the best option, but practically it will cause more trouble for White, especially under time-pressure. From a psychological perspective, this is also the best continuation, since the bishop finally joins the game.

31.♕d2? Too modest. In order to preserve the balance, White should have picked up the gauntlet: 31.fxe4,

ANALYSIS DIAGRAM

when 31...♕xf1+?! is attractive; but it doesn't work: 32.♖xf1 ♗d4 33.♕xd4+! cxd4 34.♘e2 ♖xf1+ 35.♔xf1. Now White's king is closer to the centre. 35...♔g7 36.♘xd4 ♔f6 37.♘f5 ♔e5 38.♔e2 and now 38...♖c8? would be a mistake in view of 39.d4+!.
Best is 31...♕c7! 32.♖xf8+ ♖xf8 33.b6 axb6 34.axb6 ♕d7 35.♘e2 ♕a4, and with the active bishop, Black has enough compensation.
31...e3 32.♕c2 ♗e5 33.g3 ♖de8 34.♔g2

34...♔g8?! A very logical move, but missing the key point. The best way to destroy White's defensive fortress is 34...♗xc3! 35.♕xc3+ ♔g8. Now ...e2 and ...♖e3 are unstoppable. 36.♖be1 e2 37.♖f2 ♖e3, and Black is winning.
35.♖be1
She should have played 35.♘e2!, not allowing ...e2 (after taking on c3).
35...♗xc3 36.♕xc3

36...♕xd5?
Again I missed 36...e2 37.♖f2 ♖e3.
37.♕c4 ♖f5 38.♖e2
White finally manages to hold the position and move to the next stage.
38...♔f8 39.♕c3 ♔f7 40.♕c2

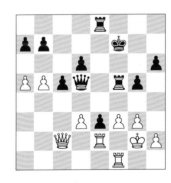

40...g4?! When time is running out, people tend to make emotional decisions... I should have played 40...h5

(41.♕c4 ♚g6). If your opponent can't do anything, it is better to be well-prepared.

41.♕c4! ♕xc4 42.dxc4 h5 43.f4?!

After the pawn structure gets fixed, the white king will find it virtually impossible to approach the passed e-pawn.

43...d5 44.cxd5 ♖xd5 45.♖c1 ♖e4 46.♖c3 c4 47.♖cxe3 ♖xe3 48.♖xe3 ♖xb5 49.♖c3 ♖xa5 50.♖xc4 ♖a2+ 51.♔g1

51...♖b2 51...b5 52.♖c5 b4 was more straightforward.

52.♖c5 ♔g6 53.♖g5+ ♔h6 54.♖g8 a5 55.f5 ♖b5

56.♖g6+
Or 56.f6 ♖f5 57.♖b8 (57.♖a8 ♔g6)

57...a4!. No rush to capture the 'dead' pawn. 58.♖xb7 ♖a5 59.♖b2 ♔g6 60.♔f2 ♔xf6, and Black wins.

56...♔h7 57.♖g5 a4 58.♖xh5+

58...♔g8 Avoiding the final trap: 58...♔g7?? 59.f6+. **59.♖g5+ ♔f7 60.♖xg4 ♖a5 61.♖d4 a3 62.♖d1 a2 63.♖a1 b5 64.g4 b4**
White resigned.

■ ■ ■

A sly trap

China had already secured a place in the final before the final round and could not be overtaken. The US managed to secure its place by beating the leader in their last encounter in the preliminaries. In that match, China's Board 1 Ding Liren won a beautiful endgame.

Ding Liren
Hikaru Nakamura
Nations Cup 2020 (10)

position after 42...♔g8

White has an extra pawn, but the opposite-coloured bishops make it a likely draw.

43.b5 ♖e4+ 44.♔f5

A sly trap. Objectively speaking, 44.♔g3 offered better winning chances.

44...g6+ Very tempting, but wrong. With 44...♗d5 Black could have kept good drawing chances. **45.♔xg6 ♗e8+ 46.♔f5 ♗xh5 47.♔xe4 ♗e2**

It looks as if Black will manage to block the white queenside pawns, but Ding Liren has looked further.

48.a4 ♗d1 49.a5 ♗e2

50.♗e5! This is the point. After White has won the c-pawn, Black no longer has a real blockade on the queenside. After 50.b6 c6 he would have.

50...♗xb5 51.♗xc7 ♔f7 52.♗d5 ♔e7 53.♔c5 ♗e2 54.♔b6 ♗f3

55.c4 ♔d7 56.c5 ♔c8 57.h4
♗e2 58.♗f4 ♗f3 59.a6 bxa6
60.♔xa6 ♔d7 61.♔b6 ♔c8
62.c6 ♗h5 63.♔c5 ♗g4 64.♔d6
♔d8 65.c7+ ♔e8 66.h5

Black resigned.

Impressive Yu Yangyi

The final between China and USA was a bit of an anti-climax, because according to the rules China had drawing odds (they had scored half a board point more in the preliminaries). When Yu Yangyi had beaten So, the issue had essentially been settled, and Caruana's victory over Wei Yi no longer mattered. Yu Yangyi was the big man on the Chinese team, scoring 7½ from 10 in total. His win against So was impressive. 'A modern masterpiece', Svidler called it. Here it is, with notes by the winner.

NOTES BY
Yu Yangyi

Yu Yangyi
Wesley So
Nations Cup 2020 (final)
Queen's Gambit Declined, Ragozin Variation

I was very happy to participate in the Online Nations Cup organized by FIDE. My team mates and I played very well and finished 1st in the preliminaries, even if we lost to the US team 1½-2½ in the last round. After Round 9, I had no idea which team we would play against in the

Yu Yangyi was the big man of the Chinese team, scoring 7½ from 10. With his final win against Wesley So, he painted 'an unforgettable picture'. (Photo taken at the Batumi Olympiad)

final. So far I hadn't watched my team mates' games, but now they suggested that I'd better do so. I kept this in mind in our Round 10 encounter with the US, when I played Wesley So. I had planned to go for the Berlin Defence, so I could make a draw and get myself some sleep before the final. But when I saw that my team mates' games all had so-so positions, I suddenly realized that I should play for a win. However, I missed a couple of chances and my opponent played very well and managed to attack my king, so I lost in the end.

And then our team had to play the US again in the final, and again my opponent was Wesley So.
1.d4 ♘f6 2.c4 e6 3.♘c3 ♗b4 4.♘f3 d5
He goes for the Ragozin Defence.
5.♕b3 I had played this before in classical games.
5...c5 6.dxc5 ♘a6
This year in Wijk aan Zee, Vishy

Anand played 6...♘c6 against me (½-½, 32).
7.cxd5 ♘xd5
And last year, Pentala Harikrishna played the variation with 7...♕a5 against me (½-½, 30).

8.c6! A new move and a new idea. I wanted to break up Black's queenside pawn structure, hoping to leave the a6-knight in an awkward position.
8...♕a5?! This will cause Black some minor problems. Perhaps 8...0-0!? or 8...bxc6 9.♕c2 would have been better.

Yu Yangyi's win against So was impressive. A modern masterpiece, Svidler called it

9.♗d2 bxc6 10.g3!

I chose to move the bishop to g2, controlling the h1-a8 diagonal rather than the f1-a6 diagonal.

After both 10.e4 ♘xc3 11.bxc3 ♗e7 and 10...♘c5 11.♕c2 ♘xc3 12.bxc3 ♗a3 the position is equal.

10...♘xc3 11.bxc3 ♗e7 12.♗g2 0-0 13.0-0

Interesting was 13.♘d4!? ♗d7 14.♗xc6 ♘c5, when Black should have compensation for the pawn.

13...e5

14.♕c2!?

I had planned to play 14.♕c4, but then I saw that Black could play 16...f6 and I was not impressed by my position: 14...♗e6 15.♕xc6 ♖ac8 16.♕e4 f6 (in fact, 16...♗f6 is better, giving Black counterchances), but I had missed that I could go 17.♘d4!.

14...♕c7 15.♕e4! f6 16.♕c4+ ♚h8 17.♗e3!

Here I felt my position was a bit better, because my queen on c4 controlled Black's bishop and the a6-knight.

17...♘b8 18.♖fd1! Here I faced a dilemma, because Black is about to play ....♗a6 and attack my pawn on e2, followed by ...♘d7. So I decided to sacrifice a pawn.

18...♗a6

19.♕e6

After 19.♕g4 f5 20.♕h5 ♗xe2 21.♖d2 g6 22.♕h6 ♗xf3 23.♗xf3 ♘d7 White has enough compensation for the pawn.

Another good square for the queen is e4: 19.♕e4 ♘d7 (19...♗xe2 20.♖d2

Nations Cup 2020 Preliminaries		1		2		3		4		5		6		TB1	TB2
1	China	*	*	2½	1½	3	2½	2	2½	2½	2½	3	3½	17	26
2	USA	1½	2½	*	*	1	1½	3	2½	2	2½	2½	3	13	22
3	Europe	1	1½	3	2½	*	*	2	2½	2½	2	2½	2	13	22
4	Russia	2	1½	1	1½	2	1½	*	*	2	2½	3	2	8	19
5	India	1½	1½	2	1½	1½	2	2	1½	*	*	1½	2½	5	18
6	Rest of the World	1	½	1½	1	1½	2	1	2	2½	1½	*	*	4	15

Nations Cup 2020 Final	
Ding Liren - Nakamura	½-½
Caruana - Wei Yi	1-0
Yu Yangyi - So	1-0
Krush - Hou Yifan	½-½
	2-2
China won on tiebreak points	

♗a6 21.♘h4 also favours White)
20.♘h4, and White is better.

19...♗xe2?!
Risky. An interesting alternative was
19...♗c8!? 20.♕c4 ♗a6, when I was
thinking of 21.♕e4 anyway.

20.♖d2
Here 20.♘h4!? was a very powerful
exchange sacrifice: 20...♗xd1
21.♖xd1, and now:
– 21...♖d8 22.♖xd8+ ♕xd8 23.♗e4!

ANALYSIS DIAGRAM

23...g6 (23...♘d7 24.♗xc6 ♘f8
25.♕f7, and the threat of 26.♘f5 is
killing) 24.♕f7, with a strong attack.
– 21...♗a3 22.♕h3, and here, too,
White's attack is strong.

20...♗a6
20...♗xf3 21.♗xf3 is really bad for
Black.

21.♘h4!?
I calculated 21.♖ad1!?, but I thought
Black could free himself after
21...♗c8 22.♕c4 ♘d7 (White
should also be better after 22...♗a6
23.♕h4 ♗c8 24.♗f1! ♗f5 25.g4 ♗e4
26.♕h3). But I missed 23.♘g5!, and
White is far better.

21...♗c8 22.♕c4 f5

23.♘f3! Eyeing the g5-square. I was
looking at 23.♖ad1, but I was afraid
that after 23...e4 my h4-knight and
g2-bishop would be blocked.

23...h6!?
I had not considered this, while calcu-
lating the variations after 23...♘d7!?
24.♘g5! at length, e.g. 24...♗xg5
25.♗xg5 ♗b7 26.a4!? ♘b6 27.♕c5 h6
28.♗e7 ♖fe8 29.♗d6 ♕f7, and White
should have enough compensation
for the pawn.

24.♖ad1 ♔h7!
The best defence, as 24...♘d7 loses
to 25.♕e6, and 24...♖f6 to 25.♘xe5
♕xe5 26.♖d8+ ♗xd8 27.♖xd8+ ♔h7
28.♕g8+ ♔g6 29.♖xc8.

25.h4!!
Very strong, preparing h5 and ♘h4.
I had also calculated 25.♗c5!?, but
this leaves White with only a minimal
plus after 25...e4 26.♘h4 (26.♘d4
♗xc5 27.♕xc5 ♖f6 is even better for
Black, since the b8-knight will come
to e5) 26...♖f6 27.♗xe7 ♕xe7 28.g4.

25...♖f6
Now Black is ready to go ...♗e6,
followed by ...♘d7. I started calcu-
lating both 26.♗g5 and 26.♘g5, and
after three minutes I decided on:

26.♘g5+!! hxg5

NIC Interactive eBooks

NEW!

We at New In Chess have been working hard to create our own digital book service. Its recent launch has instantly become a spectacular success, probably because it coincided with the start of the Corona lockdowns. Already thousands of readers are enjoying the advantages of a NIC

Interactive eBook on their PC, notebook, smartphone or tablet: it is an exact copy of the printed book, it arrives within a couple of minutes, the postman will not be ringing your door, it doesn't take up space on your bookshelves, and it allows you to replay all the games, fragments and variations on the built-in chessboard. Have look at the books that are presently available as an Interactive eBook, and don't forget to check out our website because we are adding more books every week!

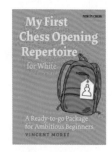
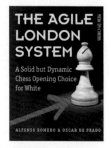
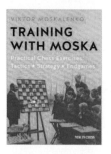
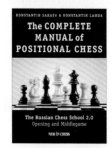

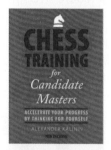
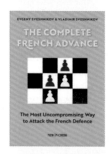

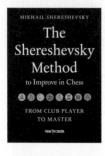

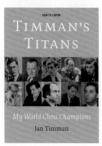

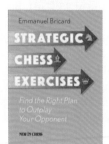

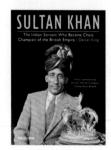

visit www.newinchess.com/books-app to view recent additions and find out about the heavily discounted **NIC Interactive eBook of the Week**

If the king moves away, 26...♔h8, White continues 27.♗c5! ♖f8 (also losing are 27...hxg5 28.hxg5 ♖f8 29.♕h4+ ♔g8 30.♗d6 ♕b7 31.♕h5 and 27...♗a6 28.♕b4 ♗xc5 29.♖d8+) 28.♗d6 ♗xd6 29.♖xd6

and now Black is lost after both 29...♕e7 30.♕c5 ♔g8 31.♗f1 and 29...hxg5 30.hxg5 f4 (30...e4 31.♕e2) 31.♗e4.

27.hxg5

27...♖g6

While Black was thinking, I quickly calculated the variations after 27...♖g6 and 27...♗a6.

After 27...♗a6 28.♕b3 ♖f8 (28...♖g6 loses to 29.♕f7 ♗c8 30.♖d4 exd4 31.♖xd4) White wins with 29.f4!! e4 30.♔f2 ♕c8 31.♖h1+ ♔g6 32.♕d1 ♖h8 33.♖d6+ ♗xd6 34.♕xd6+ ♔f7 35.♖xh8 ♕xh8 36.g6+ ♔e8 37.♗c5, and mate will follow soon.

During the game I didn't realize that Black's best defence is actually 27...♖e6!; but when I analysed the game afterwards, I found that White wins with

28.g4!! f4, e.g. 29.♗d5 fxe3 30.♗xe6 exd2 31.♕e4+ g6 32.♕h1+ ♔g7 33.♕h6 mate.

28.♗d5!!

I had the feeling that this was crushing, since there is no way for Black to stop the combined attack of ♗g8+ and ♔g2, vacating the h-file. Short of time, my opponent immediately replied:

28...f4

29.♗e4!

I felt that this was winning in view of the threats of ♕f7 and ♔g2. In the meantime, Black's queenside pieces are stuck on their original squares.

29...♗xg5 30.♖d6! ♗f6

31.♔g2!

A very nice move, allowing the rook to go to h1 with check.

31...f3+ 32.♔xf3 ♗g4+ 33.♔g2 ♗xd1 34.♖xd1

And Black resigned.

I was very happy to win this game, because So is a very competitive player. I felt I had been playing at a high level and was nervous all the time. Only later did I realize that my victory had made the score 2-1 and that I had secured the championship point, since a tie was enough for us to win the title.

This game made me feel like a good artist who always imagines himself painting an unforgettable picture! ■

MAXIMize your Tactics

with Maxim Notkin

Find the best move in the positions below

Solutions on page 91

1. White to play

2. Black to play

3. Black to play

4. White to play

5. White to play

6. Black to play

7. Black to play

8. White to play

9. White to play

CHESSBASE ACCOUNT:

Access the world of ChessBase from wherever you are 24/7!

PLAYCHESS
The ultimate chess experience

LIVE DATABASE
Professional research: 8 million games online

MY GAMES CLOUD
Your one-stop cloud storage area

FRITZ ONLINE
Your browser-based chess engine

VIDEOS
Private Masterclasses

OPENINGS
Welcome to modern opening preparation

TRAINING
Calculate, sacrifice, mate

ENGINE CLOUD
Top engine on the best hardware

LET'S CHECK
Knowledge is mate: 200 million analyses

CB NEWS
The world-renowned chess news portal

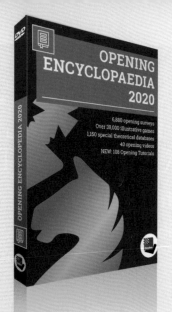

OPENING ENCYCLOPAEDIA 2020

6,880 opening surveys
Over 38,000 illustrative games
1,150 special theoretical databases
40 opening videos
NEW: 108 Opening Tutorials

The comprehensive theoretical reference work for beginners and pros alike

The new Opening Encyclopaedia 2020 is a collection of all the opening articles from all the issues of ChessBase Magazine and covers with more than 1,160 articles the whole gamut of openings. An enormous treasure trove of ideas and high-level analysis! In the new edition, as usual the number of articles has increased – compared to the previous year 70 new opening articles as well as 230 new opening surveys have been added. A lot has also been done in connection with layout and usability: the menu structure involves considerably improved access. Under the main categories "Open Games", "Semi-Open Games", "Closed Openings", "Semi-Closed Openings", "English Opening" and "Flank Openings" you will find all the articles classified according to the openings' names.

Compared to the previous edition the number of opening videos has simply been doubled! 40 selected videos with the most popular ChessBase authors – e.g. Daniel King, Simon Williams, Yannick Pelletier, Mihail Marin, Erwin l'Ami – await you. That represents a total of over 14 hours of the best chess entertainment!

And there is another important innovation: for the first time the encyclopaedia also contains opening tutorials; these are introductory texts on all known areas both for familiarisation for beginners as well an orientation for advanced players. Each opening is presented in brief, the most impor-

tant characteristics and principles are explained: do you want to play with panache or solidly? Have you already found the correct opening for you? Let us inspire you. Take a look at which opening suits you!

All innovations at a glance:

- Over 1,160 opening articles with professional analyses by prestigious title holders
- 40 opening videos by the most popular ChessBase authors – total running time: over 14 hours
- Now includes opening tutorials presenting all known openings for beginners to get to know them
- 6,888 opening surveys, 230 of which updated by GM Lubomir Ftacnik
- Database with all 38,700 games from the opening articles
- Intuitive menu structure, classification by opening name, rapid and easy access

Opening Encyclopaedia 2020   **99.90 €**

Update from
Opening Encyclopaedia 2019   **69.90 €**

ChessBase GmbH · News: en.chessbase.com · CB Shop: shop.chessbase.com
CHESSBASE DEALER: NEW IN CHESS · P.O. Box 1093 · NL-1810 KB Alkmaar
phone (+31)72 5127137 · fax (+31)72 5158234 · WWW.NEWINCHESS.COM

Thomas Willemze

Test your decision-making skills

What would you play?

Studying the games of top players undeniably helps you to get better. Yet, games played at a lower level often can be more instructive, as they are easier to relate to for most of us.

Every now and then you face an opponent to whom common chess rules do not seem to apply. These so-called *disruptive* players do not care about objective evaluations but only seek to unbalance the game and push you outside your comfort zone.

In this issue, we are going to investigate how to handle this kind of guerrilla-play by looking at a practical example from both perspectives.

I have selected four exercises, and I invite you to take your time and write down the moves that you would have played in an actual game. The first two exercises put you into the shoes of the *disrupter*. In the last two, you can use what you have learnt to find an effective remedy.

Next you can compare your answers to the game analysis on the following pages.

The Exercises

The encounter between Liam Hylands (Elo 1928) and Andrew Baruch (Elo 2076) in the current 4NCL took a normal course until Black unbalanced the game with a slightly dubious but interesting exchange sacrifice. What follows is a nerve-wrecking battle in which White tries to keep the position under control and Black does everything in his power to grab the initiative.

Exercise 1

position after 26.♕d3

We join the game shortly after the sacrifice. Black has an important decision to make. **How would you continue?** Would you cover your bishop with **26...d4** or relocate it with **26...♗e5** ?

Exercise 2

position after 31.♕b5

White's last couple of moves were very good, and he now seems to have everything under control. Black desperately needs to spice up the position. **What would you play?**

Exercise 3

position after 32...♔g6

We will now switch our perspective to the white side and find a way to keep the game under control. Black just attacked our bishop. **What would you play?** Defend it with **33.h4** or move it with **33.♗f4**?

Exercise 4

position after 35...♘h4

Black's disruptive strategy seems to have worked out well after all. He has turned the game completely upside down! Somehow, he has found a way to coordinate his queen and knight and is now threatening to mate our king with **36...♕xg2**. White did not see a way out and resigned in this position – prematurely, because he did have an opportunity to keep the game going. **Can you find it?**

Liam Hylands (1928)
Andrew Baruch (2076)
Daventry 2020
Alekhine Defence, Modern Variation

1.e4 ♘f6 2.e5 ♘d5 3.d4 d6 4.♘f3 g6 5.♗e2 ♗g7 6.0-0 0-0 7.c4 ♘b6

The black knight moves for the third time in the first seven moves. This is very typical for the Alekhine Defence. My first trainer, the late Rob Brunia, once explained that Alekhine copied this setup from Napoleon Bonaparte, who used his cavalry in war to lure the enemy soldiers within firing distance. Later I discovered that the first 1.e4 ♘f6 game in the Megabase was played in 1802 between Madame de Remusat and... Napoleon! It continues: 2.d3 ♘c6 3.f4 e5 4.fxe5 ♘xe5 5.♘c3 ♘fg4 6.d4 ♕h4+ 7.g3 ♕f6 8.♘h3 ♘f3+ 9.♔e2 ♘xd4+ 10.♔d3 ♘e5+ 11.♔xd4 ♗c5+ 12.♔xc5 ♕b6+ 13.♔d5 ♕d6 mate.

This game looks too good to be true and may have been composed, but is a clear demonstration of Napoleon's favourite strategy.

8.exd6 cxd6 9.♘c3 ♗g4

Black increases the pressure on two pawns in one move! A well-timed ...♗xf3 more or less forces White to recapture with his bishop, which means that both the c4-pawn and the d4-pawn may soon lose an important defender.

10.♗e3 ♘c6
10...♗xf3 11.♗xf3 is too hasty, since it leaves the b7-pawn under attack.

11.b3
White covers the c4-pawn, since 11...♗xf3 was in the air.

11...d5! 12.c5 ♘c8

Black's ...d6-d5 has split the board in two, leaving each player one half to focus on. White has an extra pawn on the queenside, and a logical plan would be to grab more space with b3-b4-b5. Black, for his part, will improve his position on the kingside and can always consider a well-timed ...e7-e5 to take over the centre.

13.b4!
White shows no hesitation! This direct approach is tactically justified by 13...♘xb4 14.♖b1 ♘c6 15.♖xb7.
13...♗xf3 14.♗xf3 e6 15.b5

15...♘6e7 This is bad news for the c8-knight. 15...♘a5, followed by 16...♘e7 and 17...♘f5, would have been the best way to finish development.
16.♕d2 This move allows Black to solve his knight congestion. 16.♗g4! would have been strong, since Black cannot allow 16...♘f5 17.♗xf5 gxf5.

ANALYSIS DIAGRAM

The doubled f-pawns make it very hard for Black to create anything on the kingside or in the centre, whereas White has already made a lot of progress on 'his' queenside. As a result, Black had to leave his knight on e7 on move 16, which is really bad news for its peer on c8.
16...♘f5 17.♗g4 ♘ce7

Black has found good squares for both his knights and is totally fine now.

18.♖fc1 a6 19.a4 h5 20.♗xf5 ♘xf5 21.bxa6 bxa6

The game now enters a very interesting phase. The fight for the open b-file has started!

22.♖ab1 ♕a5 23.♖b6 ♖fc8

The standard 23...♖ab8 24.♖cb1 ♖xb6 25.♖xb6, followed by a powerful blow in the centre with 25...e5!, leads to a very complex fight in which Black's chances are by no means worse.

24.♖cb1

24...♖xc5 Objectively speaking, this sacrifice leads to an advantage for White. But who cares about objective evaluations nowadays? Black was looking for an unbalanced position and that is exactly what he is going to get.

25.dxc5 ♗xc3 26.♕d3

We have arrived at **Exercise 1**. The question was: should Black cover his bishop with 26...d4, or relocate his bishop to e5?

26...d4

It makes perfect sense for Black to win back a pawn after an exchange sacrifice, but keeping his pieces well-coordinated with 26...♗e5! was more important. Black really needs an active bishop to compensate for the material deficit and his oppo-

Objectively speaking, this sacrifice leads to an advantage for White. But who cares about objective evaluations nowadays?

nent's firm control of the b-file. From e5, the bishop covers the important b8-square and keeps the dark squares around his king safe.

27.♗g5!

Well played! The black king already starts feeling the absence of its bishop.

27...♕xc5 28.♗f6

The deadly 29.♖b8+ is in the air!

28...♕c8

29.♖xa6

An excellent move, winning a pawn, but my personal favourite would be 29.♕e4, to keep the position under control and prevent Black from developing any form of counterplay. We must understand that piece activity is key for Black. He is clearly outside his comfort zone in such a passive position and we should not allow him to improve his pieces. 29.♕e4 is a real killer, since it threatens 30.♕xa8!

♕xa8 31.♖b8+ ♕xb8 32.♖xb8+ ♔h7 33.♖h8 mate. 29...♔h7 would be the most stubborn defence, but after 30.♗e5! the white rook will soon enter the back rank, with decisive effect.

29...♔h7

29...♖xa6 30.♕xa6! ♕xa6 31.♖b8+ ♔h7 32.♖h8, mate, was the idea.

30.♖xa8 ♕xa8 31.♕b5

We have arrived at **Exercise 2**. Things clearly did not work out as planned for Black and it is time to come up with something unexpected. Luckily for him, GM David Smerdon just wrote an excellent article (see New In Chess 2020/1) and book on swindling. One valuable piece of advice was to look for your opponent's weakest spot.

31...g5!

Black passed the swindling test with flying colours! The bishop was not only the most annoying piece, it is also the only undefended one, which means he can attack it! Objectively speaking, Black is still lost, but after

has been able to break the mating net around his king and pose a serious question to the white bishop. Should it stay or should it go? This was **Exercise 3**.

his promising position earlier on and focuses on making the best moves. This is extremely difficult. Not many players have the ability to hit the reset button right after their opponent has slipped through their fingers.
34.♗c7 d3 35.♕b3 ♘h4

Remember that piece activity is more important than anything when you face a disruptive player!

this highly practical move the tables will soon be turned.

31...♕e4 centralizes the queen and looks promising, but allows White to trade queens and liquidate to a winning endgame.

ANALYSIS DIAGRAM

32.♕b7! (remember this move, it will return in the final exercise!) 32...♘d6 33.♕xe4 ♘xe4 34.♗d8 d3 35.♖d1. This position still looks dangerous for White, but the truth is that Black will be unable to expel the white rook and stop the passed a-pawn at the same time.
32.♗xg5 ♔g6

At the small price of a pawn, Black

The right answer was 33.h4!, to stabilize the bishop. White is totally in control after, for instance, 33...♕e4 (33...f6 is refuted by 34.♕d7! fxg5 35.♕xe6+) 34.f3 ♕c2 35.♖c1 ♕a2 36.♕e5.

ANALYSIS DIAGRAM

33.♗f4
This move leaves the bishop unprotected and allows Black to improve his most important piece with tempo.
33...♕e4!

My engine still favours White, but does not understand chess psychology. Black is clearly back in his comfort zone and it already feels as if he is taking over. White can only break the momentum if he forgets about

It is hard to believe that only six moves ago White's dominant major pieces and strong bishop ruled the board. Impressed by Black's threats and not seeing a way out, White resigned.

White played a good game, but had difficulties adjusting to the rapidly changing circumstances. If he had been able to forget the past, he would probably have found the correct answer to **Exercise 4**: 36.♕b7!.

White is not worse after, for instance, 36...♕xa4 37.♖f1 d2 38.♕b1+! ♔g5 39.♕d3.

Conclusion
This game demonstrated how you should always be ready to push the reset button and adjust to rapidly changing circumstances in your games. Also remember that piece activity is of prime importance when you face a disruptive player! ■

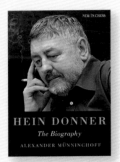

Hein Donner – The Biography
Alexander Münninghoff

"A fascinating insight into one of the most colourful characters in the chess world of that time and also an ideal complement to Donner's own writings in *The King*."
Steve Giddins, co-author of 'Side-Stepping Mainline Theory'

"One of my five favourite chess books."
Bent Larsen

A Skeptic's Guide to Getting Better at Chess
Willy Hendriks

After his award-winning *Move First, Think Later*, Willy Hendriks strikes again. In this ground-breaking (and very funny) investigative journey he questions the reputations of the chess greats of the past. Never before has the study of the history of chess been so entertaining and rewarding.

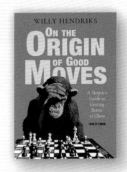

The Modern Way to Get the Upper Hand in Chess
Dmitry Kryavkin

GM Dmitry Kryakvin shows how the attack on the g-file can be used to defeat Black in a number of important Closed and Semi-Closed Defences and Flank Openings: the Dutch, the Queen's Gambit, the Nimzo-Indian, the King's Indian, the Slav and several variations of the English Opening. With lots of instructive examples.

"A veritable potpourri of aggressive ideas to spice up your openings." – *John Upham, British Chess News*

Practical Tips to Strengthen Your Mindset at the Board
Werner Schweitzer

Just like technical chess skills, mental toughness can be trained. Unlock the full power of your brain with professional mental coach and chess player Werner Schweitzer, who has been working with chess teams and individual players for many years. His lessons and simple mental workouts will help players of all levels to win more games.

Practical Endgames Exercises for Every Chess Player
Jesus de la Villa

"I love this book! In order to master endgame principles you will need to practice them."
NM Han Schut, Chess.com

"The perfect supplement to De la Villa's manual. To gain sufficient knowledge of theoretical endgames you really only need two books."
IM Herman Grooten, Schaaksite

Sultan Khan – Chess Champion of the British Empire
Daniel King

In 1929, only three years after learning the rules of chess, Sultan Khan created a sensation by becoming the British Empire champion. In 1933 he departed again for India.

"A fantastic addition to chess literature."
GM Matthew Sadler

"King offers a lot more than just the games."
Richard James, British Chess News

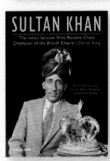

A Solid and Straightforward Chess Opening Repertoire for White
Christof Sielecki

Sielecki's repertoire with 1.d4 may be even easier to master than his 1.e4 recommendations.

"A repertoire that packs a punch."
Miguel Ararat, Florida Chess Magazine

"A host of interesting new and dangerous ideas."
John Upham, British Chess News

A Deceptively Dangerous Universal Chess Opening System for Black
Alessio De Santis

"Little short of a revelation. De Santis really has come at his subject from all conceivable angles to leave no stone unturned. Did you know that the hippopotamus is the most dangerous of all large animals? In chess opening terms, I would argue that it's also the case."
GM Glenn Flear

"Presents a very good view on the many ideas that the Hippopotamus offers." – *IM Dirk Schuh*

AlphaZero's Groundbreaking Chess Strategies and the Promise of AI
Matthew Sadler & Natasha Regan
ECF 2019 Book of the Year

"Once you experience the power of these ideas in your own game, you realise how much we can learn from the playing style of AlphaZero."
IM Stefan Kuipers

"I absolutely love it. A fascinating read: provocative, inspiring, instructive and joyful." – *GM Daniel King*

The Key to Better Calculation
Charles Hertan
Chess Café Book of the Year 2008

New Edition of the award-winning classic: 50 extra pages!

"I love this book." – *Elisabeth Vicary, USCF Online*

"When the clock is ticking away, and you have too many viable candidate moves to choose from, remember Hertan's advice."
Steve Goldberg, ChessCafe

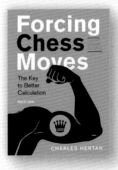

The Blitz Whisperer
Maxim Dlugy

See you later, Alireza?

In the past few months a new speed chess rivalry has grown that is getting everyone talking. The amazing 16-year-old super-star Alireza Firouzja from Iran, currently playing under the FIDE flag, has in his nonchalant manner emerged as a serious threat to Magnus Carlsen's supremacy in blitz circles. Although Alireza is rated 'only' 21st in the world in classical chess, and even lower in both blitz and rapid, he shocked the world by beating Magnus in a 194(!) game bullet marathon (1 minute per player per game) with the score of 103½-90½.

Alireza's victory felt like a sweet revenge, as everyone still remembered the controversial finish of their game in the World Blitz Championship last December, when the youngster lost on time with a bishop and three pawns versus his opponent's lonely bishop (see New In Chess 2020/1).

Only 11 days after Firouzja's sensational bullet victory, Magnus showed that he had no wish to stay defeated for very long when he met him again in the final of the Banter Blitz Cup sponsored by Chess24.com, the site the World Champion supports and co-owns. Both players got to the finals by destroying their respective opponents in a field of more than 130 strong players vying for blitz supremacy. Although the rules were quite different from regular tournaments – as the players had to live stream their games while continuously commenting on them – no one doubted that this was a most prestigious high-quality match-up.

But again, the final score was a surprising 8½-7½ win for Alireza

While for the moment Magnus Carlsen is firmly ensconced on his throne, the pundits like to speculate who will one day replace him. Following two startling upsets, **MAXIM DLUGY** examines why 16-year-old Alireza Firouzja is such a tough opponent for the Norwegian in speed chess.

Firouzja, who was never behind in this extremely close match and pocketed the $14,000 first prize. The loss got Magnus thinking how to exact revenge on the youngster and he came up with the idea to invite Alireza to the Magnus Carlsen Invitational. There, finally, Magnus did get his revenge, albeit in rapid games, with a close win of 2½-1½.

It is pretty clear that someone who is about to break into the Top 20 at age 16 is going to be a serious factor in the chess world in the next few years. Still, it's a legitimate question what makes Alireza such an uncomfortable opponent for the World Champion? To answer this question, I decided to analyse the blitz profiles of these two amazing players, hoping to come up with a list of possible reasons.

Let's dive right into their games to see in which positions these players tend to make mistakes.

Magnus Carlsen
Alireza Firouzja
Chess24 Banter Blitz Cup 2020 (1)
Queen's Gambit Declined, Ragozin Variation
1.d4 ♘f6 2.♘f3 d5 3.c4 e6 4.♘c3 ♗b4 5.cxd5 exd5 6.♗g5 0-0 7.e3 h6 8.♗h4 ♗f5 9.♕b3 ♗xc3+ 10.♕xc3 g5 11.♗g3 ♘e4 12.♕a3 ♘c6

This move is a novelty, though not a particularly great one. It shows that unlike some young players Alireza is not as concentrated on remembering

opening theory and relies mostly on his intuition. This is generally a good thing for blitz play as it produces quick decisions.

13.♗b5 Personally, I like 13.♘d2 instead, to get rid of the scary knight on e4 as soon as possible (White need not be afraid of 13...♘xd2 14.♗xd2, as this would leave him with the bishop pair and good attacking chances).

13...♘e7 14.♘d2 c6 15.♗d3 Keeping the bishop pair with 15.♗e2 was preferable, but Magnus chooses to simplify.

15...♘xd2 16.♔xd2 ♗xd3 17.♕xd3 ♕a5+ 18.♔e2 f5

One of Alireza's strong points is his uncompromising ability to go for the most aggressive continuation no matter who he is playing. This is of course partially due to his young age, which in this case is clearly helping his sense of initiative.

19.♗d6 ♖ae8

20.g4?!
A better way to pry open, or alternatively keep closed the files, would be 20.h4!, when the idea is to meet 20...g4 with 21.h5 and establish the bishop on e5 with a positional advantage.

Perhaps a key moment in their rivalry: the game that Alireza Firouzja, with a winning position, lost on time against Magnus Carlsen at the 2019 World Blitz in Moscow.

20...♖f6! An excellent response, preparing the next counter.

21.♗e5 ♘g6! Black needed to find a way to get rid of the white bishop and now White will need to be very careful to keep the balance.

22.h4! Magnus finds the best move, trying to overload the knight.

22...♘xe5
Even stronger was 22...fxg4! 23.hxg5 ♖xe5 24.dxe5 ♘xe5 25.♕c2 ♕b5+ 26.♔d1 hxg5 27.♕h7+ ♔f8 and Black's counterplay is extremely dangerous.

23.dxe5 ♖xe5 24.hxg5 hxg5 25.♖h5
This move looks strong, but pushing Black's pieces back with 25.♕d4! was more efficient. Now a critical position is about to arise.

25...♕b4 26.♖xg5+ ♔f7

27.b3?
If Magnus had noticed Black's reply, he would definitely have preferred a queen trade after either 27.♕b3 or 27.♕c3, with an even endgame. Now he is in for a shocker!

27...♕f4

Alireza Firouzja has in his nonchalant manner emerged as a serious threat to Magnus Carlsen's supremacy in blitz circles.

During the 'Banter' Alireza figured this already wins, and in fact it is extremely difficult to find the only move for White in this position in a blitz game. You can stop reading now to try and accept the challenge.

28.♕xf5?

This loses, but all reasonable looking moves seem to fail as well. All except one! After the counter-blow 28.♕c3!! White holds. The best for Black seems to be 28...♕xg5 29.♕xe5 ♕xg4+ 30.f3 ♕g2+ 31.♔d3 f4 32.♕c7+ ♔g6 33.♕d8 and White's agile queen provides enough of a safety net to save this position.

28...♕xg5 29.♕xg5 ♖xg5

And Black went on to win. (0-1, 67)

In this game, we saw a display of Alireza's intuition and strong play with the initiative. He showed his ability to quickly see tactical tricks and excellent speed in finishing off his opponents in technically winning positions.

After a draw in the second game, Magnus managed to level the score in Game 3.

Magnus Carlsen
Alireza Firouzja
Chess24 Banter Blitz Cup 2020 (3)
Ruy Lopez, Anderssen Variation

1.e4 e5 2.♘f3 ♘c6 3.♗b5 a6 4.♗a4 ♘f6 5.d3 b5 6.♗b3 ♗c5 7.c3 d6 8.♗g5 h6 9.♗h4 ♗b6 10.♘bd2 ♖b8 11.♘f1 ♘e7 12.♗xf6 gxf6 13.♘h4

13...♗e6

Once again Alireza makes the first new move. In Alekseev-Sanal, White was slightly better after 13...h5. The position looks pretty suspect for Black in either case, and Alireza was quick to recognize this himself changing his opening in the subsequent games. Still, one thing is clear – the position is sharp and certainly White will have to play in crisp fashion to prove his advantage.

14.♕h5?

A serious glitch. Black's light squares reek, and White's queen need not be on the first lines of the offensive to prove this point.

After the correct 14.♘e3 h5 15.0-0 a5 16.d4 a4 17.♗c2 it's pretty clear that White does not need to stop ...h5 to stand better.

14...♔d7!

With the black queen now going to g5, Black will win important time to bring his pieces into action.

15.♘e3 ♕g8 16.g3

The teenager is forcing him to play crazy uncontrollable positions where everything hinges on making the correct tactical decisions in the shortest periods of time.

16...♕g5 Even clearer was the immediate 16...♗xe3 17.♗xe6+! (17. fxe3 ♗g4 18.♕xf7 ♕g5 would leave White holding the loser's bag) 17... fxe6 18.fxe3 ♕g5 19.♕e2 f5 and Black is a little better.

17.♕e2 a5

Alireza continues to play uncompromisingly. The engines prefer to take some space on the kingside with 17... h5 with a balanced position.

18.♘f3 ♕g6 19.♘h4 ♕g5

20.d4!?

Magnus goes for complications instead of playing a manoeuvring game with something like 20.♗c2.

20...exd4 21.cxd4 ♗xd4 22.♘f3 ♕c5 23.0-0 ♗xe3 24.fxe3

24...a4?

Black misses a nice ploy to force some desirable trades with 24...♗c4! 25.♗xc4 ♕xc4, when Magnus would be in a tight spot as keeping the queens on the board would mean he has to seek compensation for two pawns.

25.♖ac1

25...♕b4?

This reasonable-looking move turns out to be a decisive mistake. Black's queen will now be forced into nowhere land, which will give White an immediately decisive attack.

Black had a number of reasonable replies, including 25...♕b6 and 25...♕h5, which actually make sense, with an equal position. Alireza's motto – to move forward no matter what – plays a bad joke on him in this situation.

26.♗xe6+ fxe6 27.♘d4!

The threats of ♕g4 and ♖xf6 are impossible to stop now.

27...c5 28.a3 ♕a5 29.♖xf6 cxd4

30.♕g4! ♕d2 31.♕xe6+ ♔e8 32.♖c7 ♕xe3+ 33.♔g2 ♖h7 34.♕d7

Mate.

Once again we saw Alireza not too worried about deep opening knowledge. His natural feel managed to get him out of trouble rather quickly, as Magnus misplayed his hand. With his continued attempts to play only the most aggressive moves, he missed the fact that the queen was badly needed as a defensive resource on the other side of the board.

In the next, completely uncompromising battle we can see exactly why Alireza Firouzja is such a difficult opponent for Magnus Carlsen. While Magnus prefers quiet positions where he can build up his game, the teenager is forcing him to play crazy uncontrollable positions where everything hinges on making the correct tactical decisions in the shortest periods of time. Considering that the bullet marathon showed that Alireza is at the very least a slightly faster player, these kinds of positions will obviously tend to favour the youngster.

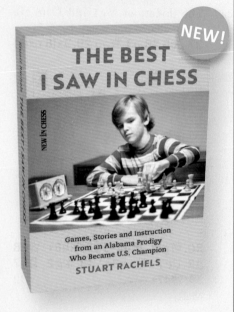
Magnus Carlsen
Alireza Firouzja
Chess24 Banter Blitz Cup 2020 (7)
King's Indian Attack

1.e4 c5 2.♘f3 e6 3.g3 ♘c6
4.♗g2 ♘f6 5.d3 d5 6.♕e2 ♗e7
7.e5 ♘d7 8.c4 ♕c7 9.cxd5 exd5
10.♘c3 ♘b6

Alireza Firouzja: always intent on playin the most explosive kind of chess possible

Though it may look like Black is playing extremely provocatively, there doesn't seem to be an immediate refutation of Black's play. Also White cannot create a comfortable easy-flow position where the moves play by themselves.

11.♗f4 ♗e6 12.h4

12...♕d7!

An excellent move, preparing ...♗g4 in some cases while moving the queen away from a possible ♘b5 attack.

13.0-0 h6

Alireza's mark! Most strong players would simply castle kingside with an absolutely beautiful position, but Black is intent on playing the most explosive kind of chess possible. He wants to castle queenside and start crazy complications!

14.♕d2 0-0-0 15.a4

15...a5?!

Without any hesitation Firouzja creates an amazing outpost for White's knight on b5.

A classically tutored player would likely play 15...d4, to give the knight the d5-square, followed by ...♗h3 to weaken White's attacking and defensive chances, with a good position.

16.♘b5 g5 17.hxg5 hxg5
18.♘xg5 ♗xg5 19.♗xg5 ♗h3

The bluff is on and Alireza simply doesn't care. White now has a very strong in-between-move that would ruin Black's chances. See if you can find it.

20.f4?

With time on the clock it would have been quite easy for Magnus to play the typical 20.e6 ♕xe6 21.♖fe1 ♕g4 22.♕f4, with a winning position. Now the game becomes completely random.

20...♗xg2 21.♕xg2 ♖dg8

22.♗f6

A very strange move by Magnus, letting the rooks combine in the attack. Instead, 22.♖ac1 would have kept the pressure.

22...♖h6

One of the rare slip ups in such positions for Firouzja. After the most aggressive and logical 22...♖h3 23.♔f2 ♕g4 Black would take over the initiative.

23.♔f2

It seems Magnus was already thinking about evacuation on the previous move. Otherwise, 23.f5!, blocking out the queen, would have been played.

23...♖hg6 23...♘b4! was extremely strong.

24.♗h4 ♔b8

25.♖ac1

In this crazy position, with only seconds on the clock, White could have controlled the board with the resounding 25.♕f3!. Now he starts losing material.

25...♘b4! 26.♕f3 ♘xa4 27.♘d6 ♘xb2 28.♖c3

28...♖xd6

This simplifying move is played to make the subsequent moves easier to find. Instead, 28...f6!! simply blows up White's position.

29.exd6 ♕xd6 30.♖b3

30...♘a4

30...c4!, preparing ...♘xd3+, was brutal, but now it's a matter of speed.

31.♖a1 b5 32.♕e2 c4 33.dxc4 dxc4 34.♖e3 ♘c5 35.♖xa5 ♘cd3+ 36.♔f1 ♕c6 37.♕f3 ♘d5 38.♖xd3 cxd3 39.♕xd3 ♘c7

40.♔f2??

The final mistake, with a few seconds on the clock. White would be OK after 40.♖a3!.

40...♕b6+ 41.♔g2 ♕xa5 42.♗f6 ♕a8+ 43.♔f2 ♕c6 44.♗e5 ♔b7 45.♕b3 ♘d5 46.♕a3 ♖c8 47.♕f3 ♕c2+ White resigned.

The positives and the negatives

This game clearly showed all the positive and negative attributes of Alireza's blitz style. His nonchalant opening preparation coupled with quick decision-making regarding the playability of different complicated middlegames with a propensity towards complications, gives him excellent chances to force his opponents into a thinking frenzy. Even if his opponent is Magnus – he doesn't change his style, as he simply doesn't yet have another one.

To beat him at blitz, Magnus has to control the opening play and try to push Alireza into technical, dry positions. The problem is – Magnus also wants to have fun and in such an environment Alireza will remain a difficult opponent for him in shorter time controls. As Alireza learns more about chess – and from what I understand that's exactly what he is doing right now – just like my good friend Vishy Anand, he will mature into a dangerous player at any time-control. ■

Provoking the pawn

A loss of time that brings positional gains. This can happen when a bishop tempts an opponent's pawn to advance.

Magnus Carlsen
Vladislav Kovalev
Wijk aan Zee 2020

1.d4 ♘f6 2.c4 e6 3.♘f3 d5 4.♘c3 ♗e7 5.♗g5 0-0 6.e3 h6

Tartakower introduced this zwischenzug in 1922 to avoid the dangers of the Marshall Attack, which arises after 6...b6 7.cxd5 exd5 8.♗d3 ♗b7 9.♗xf6 ♗xf6 10.h4. With the pawn on h6 there would no longer be the threat of ♗xh7+. **7.♗f4!?** Withdrawing to a square where the bishop could have gone in one move and thus granting Black the extra move ...h7-h6. White sort of claims that this will be rather a disadvantage for Black! **7... c5** 7...♘bd7 8.g4!?, immediately reaching for the new-born hook on h6, was Grischuk-Caruana, 2015. 7...

b6 has been played by Tartakower. With the text-move Black heads for a well-known position with a pawn-move up. **8.dxc5 ♗xc5 9.a3 ♘c6 10.♕c2** With Black's h-pawn on h7 this position is the well-known theoretical one that arises after 1.d4 ♘f6 2.c4 e6 3.♘f3 d5 4.♘c3 ♗e7 5.♗f4 0-0 6.e3 c5 7.dxc5 ♗xc5 8.a3 ♘c6 9.♕c2. **10...♘h5** Kovalev sidesteps the theoretical discussion. After 10...♕a5 (the main move in the lines without ...h7-h6) he would have to find out where the move ...h6 helps White in the attack. 11.0-0-0 followed by g2-g4 springs to mind, whereas it is doubtful if Dubov's sidestep 11.♖a2 will be repeated (11...♘e4!). Meanwhile, the text also tries to prove the usefulness of the inclusion of ...h6: ♗f4-g5 is ruled out. **11.♗g3 dxc4 12.♗xc4 ♗e7 13.♗a2!?**

A straightforward move – Carlsen is determined to prove that Black's kingside has been weakened due to ...h7-h6. **13...a6?** Valuable loss of time. **14.♖d1 ♕a5 15.♗b1 f5** An ugly move, probably the result of dismissing 15...♘f6 16.0-0 and 15...g6, which creates a new target, which White may even immediately aim for with the blunt 16.♘h4!?. **16.0-0 ♘xg3 17.hxg3 ♗f6**

18.e4! Foreseeing a tough battle with a bad pawnstructure and bad development, Kovalev now grabbed a pawn: **18...♗xc3 19.bxc3 ♕xa3** But Carlsen comfortably hauled in the full point after **20.exf5 exf5 21.♖fe1 ♕a5 22.g4** (1-0, 37).

Bishop moves that provoke pawn moves actually happen a lot. Here is a more general pattern, similar to Carlsen's game.

Johan van Mil
Stefan Reschke
Lugano 1989

position after 15...♕b8

16.♗g5 h6 17.♗c1!? White has intentionally provoked ...h6. The general idea is to set up a battery with ♕d3 and then exchange the f6-knight. Black can no longer block the ♗b1-♕d3 battery with ...g7-g6, as the h6-pawn will fall. Here the less sophisticated 17.♗h4 is strong as well as Black cannot free his position by means of exchanges: 17...♘d5? (17...♘h5? 18.d5) 18.♘xd5 ♖xd5 19.♕d3 g6 20.♗g3 ♗d6 21.♖xe6. **17...♖d7?** After 17...♗f8 Black has safeguarded his h6-pawn in time. The text-move allows White to carry out his idea without hindrance. **18.d5! ♘xd5**

19.♘xd5 19.♕c2 g6 20.♖xe6 was even stronger when Black is 'lucky' to have 20...♘f4 21.♖xd7 ♘xe6, yet the simple 22.♗a2 is devastating. **19...♖xd5 20.♖xd5 exd5 21.♕d3 g6 22.♗xh6** Plan succeeded. **22...♕d6**

23.h4! And White continued to tear Black's kingside apart (1-0, 43).

In the following game Tal also prepared a ♗c2/♕d3 battery when he provoked his opponent to play ...h7-h6.

And now Mikhail Tal went on to win with an incredibly Zen move

Mikhail Tal
Janos Flesch
Lvov 1981

position after 11...0-0

12.♗g5 h6 13.♗f4 Earlier Flesch had faced the immediate 12.♗f4. He may have been confident to repeat this with his extra pawn move. **13...♘b6 14.♗c2** There we go! The tempting 14.♕d2 can be met by 14...♘fd5 15.♗xh6 gxh6 16.♕xh6 f5 and it seems White has to be satisfied with a draw. **14...♘bd5** 14...♘fd5 15.♗e5 f6 now fails to 16.♕d3 and Black would love to have his pawn back on h7 to be able to play ...g7-g6. **15.♗e5 ♕b6 16.♕d3!?** Very inventive! And provocative as well! **16...♘b4 17.♕d2 ♘xc2 18.♗xf6 ♘xa1 19.♘h5 e5! 20.dxe5 g5**

21.e6! Tal also creates more mobility for his bishop at the cost of a pawn. **21...♕xe6** And White went on to win after the incredibly Zen move **22.h3!?** Instead, the natural 22.♗c3 seems to do the trick too, e.g.: 22...f6 23.♖xa1 ♗d7 24.♘xf6+ ♖xf6 25.♗xf6 (1-0, 32).

And here's a similar manoeuvre, equally effective, but now in Andersson style.

Ulf Andersson
Ferdinand Hellers
Haninge 1993 (match-3)

position after 14.a3

14...♘h5? 15.♗b5! c6 16.♗f1 Andersson may now direct a knight to d6 or go for the b6-pawn with a4-a5, all because the c7-pawn has advanced. **16...f6 17.♗e3 ♖ad8 18.♖ad1 ♕e7 19.♘c4 ♘f8 20.♖xd8** 20.a4 immediately is more natural, but Andersson remains on top. **20...♖xd8 21.♖d1 ♘e6 22.♖xd8+ ♕xd8 23.a4 ♗f8 24.♕a2 ♘hg7 25.a5 c5**

26.bxc5 Now Hellers eventually escaped (½-½, 37). White should not have been afraid of 26.b5 ♗xe4 and gone after the b6-pawn, 27.axb6 axb6 28.♕a7, as Black cannot easily build an attack.

Conclusion

A simple pawn move like ...h6, provoked by a teasing bishop, may lead to a change in the position with considerable consequences. When you play it (or provoke it) you should know what you are doing. ∎

Judit Polgar

Kortchnoi's lessons

Viktor Kortchnoi is one of the great modern legends and one of the most successful players never to win the world title. **JUDIT POLGAR** remembers his unparalleled passion and his unfailing will to win.

It is hard to think of a player who had a longer career than Viktor Kortchnoi (1931-2016). He won the Soviet Championship at the age of 30, had his best results between the age of 40 and 50, and remained a fearsome opponent even in his 70s and 80s.

I became aware of Kortchnoi's extraordinary fighting spirit, his **Trademark 1** (and maybe his most important one) in our first-ever game, in the Dutch League in Hilversum in 1989. I was 13 at the time and I was amazed by his immense and insatiable wish to fight. He would constantly search for his best chances, slim as they might be, and irrespective of the objective assessment of his position.

He seems to have been less than impressed by the skills of the girl he had played, because shortly afterwards, in an interview, he called me 'a coffee-house player'. Kortchnoi was famous for his sarcastic, even malicious way of criticizing others. Not everybody appreciated this, but I would call this 'Viktor's way'!

Anyway, the dramatic final phase of the game we played in Vienna in 1996 is a good example of his fighting spirit:

Viktor Kortchnoi
Judit Polgar
Vienna 1996

position after 69...♔h7

We had had one of our usual strategical and tactical King's Indian battles, with the advantage passing from one player to the other. Deep into the seventh hour of play and with just a few pieces on the board, the tension had not abated one single bit. Even though my b-pawn will inevitably promote, Kortchnoi had confidently gone for this position, knowing that he could not be worse, since his pawns and pieces were threatening, too.

70.♘f5? This sets up a little combination leading only to a draw, though.

Amazingly, 70.♔f7! would have won in study-like style, but finding all the right ideas was virtually impossible after such a long fight. The analysis below only proves that Kortchnoi was intuitively right: 70...♘d8+ 71.♔f8 ♘e6+ 72.♔e7! b1♕ 73.♔xe6.

ANALYSIS DIAGRAM

Black has a huge material advantage, but in the long run I cannot prevent one of the white pawns from queening due to White's perfect coordination: 73...♕b6+ (73...♕b3+ is parried by 74.♘d5) 74.♔e7 ♕b4+ 75.♔f7 ♕b8 76.♘f5!, with the fantastic threat of 77.g8♕+ ♕xg8+ 78.♔e7, and I would have no checks, since both g7 and g5 are defended. But 77.♘e7 is not a threat, because after 77...♕g8!!+ 78.♘xg8 the game ends in stalemate! 76...♕b3+ 77.♔e7 ♕f7+!?

I was 13 at the time and I was amazed by his immense and insatiable wish to fight

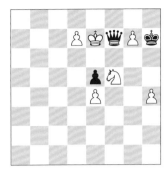

ANALYSIS DIAGRAM

Hoping for stalemate (if 77...♕a3+ then 78.♘d6 ♕a7 79.♔e8 ♕a4 80.♔f8! ♕a8+ 81.d8♕!!. A fantastic move, don't you think? 81...♕xd8+ 82.♘e8. Once again, the queen is useless. The knight covers the king against checks on d6 or f6 and the reserve pawns control d5 and g5, ensuring the promotion) 78.♔d6 ♕g8 (78...♕f6+ 79.♘c7 ♕f7 runs into the little combination 80.g8♕+! ♔xg8 81.♘h6+, winning).

ANALYSIS DIAGRAM

79.♘e7! (playing for zugzwang with 79.h5? unexpectedly frees the queen: 79...♕a2! 80.d8♕ ♕e6+! (with the h-pawn controlling g6, Black saves the game by stalemate!) 81.♔c5 ♕c8+!) 79...♕b8+ 80.♔e6 ♔xg7

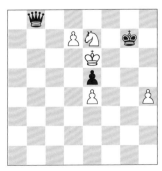

ANALYSIS DIAGRAM

Viktor Kortchnoi never tired of trying to deepen his chess understanding.

81.♘c6!. The last touch. White threatens d8♕ and the checks will soon run out: 81...♕b3+ (81...♕g8+ 82.♔xe5+−) 82.♔d6 ♕a3+ 83.♔c7, and White wins. There is no more check and what's worse, I cannot even pin the pawn with ...♕e7! What an amazing joint effort by the small white army!

70...b1♕ 71.g8♕+ ♔xg8 72.♘e7+ ♔h7 73.♘xc6 ♕xe4! The only adequate defence, forcing an immediate draw in view of 74.d8♕ ♕xh4+.

In 1995, at the magical age of 64, Kortchnoi won a strong tournament in Madrid. He explained his success saying: 'I had to win, otherwise people would start to forget me...' This reveals **Trademark 2**, his inexhaustible passion for chess and taught me that, no matter how successful you have been in your best years, you need to maintain a never-ceasing inner wish and impulse to continue performing as well as you can!

I am confident that Viktor was the most fanatical chess player I have ever met. Despite his advancing age, he never lost his appetite for studying and trying out new ideas. Knowing that he did not like working with computers, one would think that at some point his research efforts would start facing practical problems. However, he could rely on a small but faithful 'team', which included

his wife Petra who, besides helping him in everyday matters, prepared chess material for him with the help of a computer.

My feeling was that Kortchnoi aimed at something higher than just reminding people of his impressive 'business card'. I believe that he wanted to be admired and respected for what he was still able to do after so many years in the world chess arena.

In Madrid 1995, I managed to win a good last-round game against him, which did not deprive him from winning.

**Judit Polgar
Viktor Kortchnoi**
Madrid 1995

position after 41...♔h8

With my previous few moves I had been checking his king on the eighth and seventh ranks to little effect. With my next move, I decided to centralize my queen.

42.♕c5 ♚h7 It appears that the king has to evacuate the h8-square even without being under attack, because after 42...e3?, 43.♗xe3! ♕xe3? 44.♕f8+ will be mate.

43.♗e3! I am very happy about my bishop play in this game. When the rooks were still on the board, the calm retreat ♗g5-c1 had ensured my king's safety and cleared the g-file for my attack. After a period of hibernation, the bishop moves again in order to block the passed pawn.

43...♕f6 Aiming for counterplay.

44.♕a7+! Under the changed circumstances this check is more effective, since the king is forced to advance.

44...♚g6

The point is that if 44...♚g8?, 45.h7+ ♚h8 46.♗d4 wins the queen.

45.♗c1! Another subtle move, not only defending the back rank but also clearing the g1-a7 diagonal.

45...♕e5 46.♕g1+! My queen follows the bishop's example by executing a long retreat. Such elegant moves are sometimes hard to see.

He would always choose the most principled continuation, no matter how risky or complicated it might seem

46...♚h7 47.♕g5

47...♕xg5

There is nothing better already.

If 47...♕c7, 48.♕f5+ wins the e4-pawn. 47...♕d4 48.♕f5+ yields me a decisive attack: 48...♚h8 49.♕f8+ ♚h7 50.♕f7+ ♚h8 51.a4! bxa4 (otherwise the a-pawn would decide) 52.c4 ♘b6 (the knight does not have good squares. If 52...♘e3, 53.♕g7+ or 52...♘b4 53.♕f8+ wins the knight) 53.♗d2 ♕d3+ 54.♚a1, and there is no defence against ♗c3+.

48.♗xg5

Without the queens, the win is relatively simple.

48...c5 49.♚c1 c4 50.a3 ♚g6 51.♚d2 ♚h7 52.b3 cxb3 53.cxb3 ♚g6 54.♗e3

And, confronted with the slow advance of my a-pawn, Kortchnoi resigned.

Our games usually resembled a roller coaster, with ups and downs and lots of excitement. I used to work hard to prepare for my games against him, although I expected that he would come up with a new and interesting idea that would lead to sharp play. I was also aware of the fact that he would always choose the most principled continuation at the crucial moment, no matter how risky or complicated it might seem. I would define this as **Trademark 3**, his over-the-board ambition and courage.

I was, nevertheless, convinced that if I stayed alert, I would get at least one opportunity to change the course of the

game in my favour. Here is an example in which that did not fully apply, but my paradoxical idea will surely bring about some smiles.

**Viktor Kortchnoi
Judit Polgar**
Hoogeveen 2001 (2)

position after 21...♕h5

I knew that my position was hopeless but I found a fun move:

21...b3!?

As if I had not enough problems already, I also left my queen *en prise*!

22.♗e2 As surprised as he might have been, Kortchnoi did not lose his composure and continued developing. My trick consisted of 22.♗xa5? ♗b4+ 23.♚d1 ♖e1 mate.

For the truth's sake, the simpler 22.♘xe8 wins, too.

22...b2 23.♖b1 ♗b4 24.0-0 ♖e7 25.♗h6 White maintains his kingside domination and, since my rooks are hanging, his extra pawn will decide. I resigned 15 moves later.

Conclusion

Summing up, the qualities I admired in Viktor Kortchnoi and that inspired me were:

■ His unrelenting fighting spirit to the happy or bitter end, regardless.

■ His unparallelled passion for chess that bordered fanaticism.

■ His over-the-board creativity, ambition and courage. ■

1. Yu Yangyi-Korobov
chess.com 2020

40.♕xf8+! Invitation to a beheading. Black resigned on account of 40...♔xf8 41.♖d8+ ♔e7 42.♖e8 mate.

2. Horvath-Balashov
Prague 2020

44...♖h1+! 45.♔xh1 ♕f1+ 46.♔h2 Or 46.♖g1 ♕h3 mate. **46...f3+ 47.♔g3 ♕g2** Mate.

3. Byklum-Predojevic
Norway tt 2020

Should Black exchange the queens? No! **25...♘xf3! 26.♕xe7 ♘f2+! 27.♖xf2 ♖g1** Mate.

4. Antipov-Varga
Budapest 2012

Black looks comfortable if it were not for one small nuisance: **14.♗xc6+! bxc6** On any other move, 15.♗b5 traps the queen. **15.♘d6+ ♗xd6 16.♕xa6** Black resigned.

5. Aryan-Buksa
Moscow 2020

58.♕h8+ ♔g5 59.f4+! ♔xf4 60.♕h4+ ♔e5 61.♕e7+ This was all forced. Only now Black has a choice – but a sad one. 61...♔d5 62.♕b7+ loses the queen, and **61...♔f4 62.♕e3** is mate.

6. Van Haastert-Warakomski
Amsterdam 2020

30...♖h1+! 31.♔xh1 ♕h6+ 32.♕h3 A more elegant loss was 32.♔g1 ♕e3+ 33.♔f1 ♖h8! and there is no defence against ...♖h1 mate. **32...♘f2+ 33.♔g1 ♘xh3+** White resigned.

7. Tabatabaei-Kotronias
Gibraltar 2020

21...♖f4! Creating a deadly threat and also preventing a queen check on h4. White resigned – he loses too much material after 22.♕xe7+ ♔h6 23.f3 (or 23.♕xe6 ♖e4+) 23...♕e3+ 24.♔f1 ♕xc1+ and 25...♖xh1 while if 24.♔d1 then 24...♖d4+ 25.♔c2 ♕d3 mate.

8. Zhao-Kritz
Pawtucket 2008

22.♕g6! ♕e3+ 22...♘f6 23.♖xf6 or 22...f5 23.exf6 or 22...♕xb2+ 23.♔d2 just hasten the end. **23.♔d1 fxg6 24.♖xf8+ ♔h7 25.h5!** Black is forced to give up the queen in order to prevent mate on g6: **25...♕xd3+ 26.cxd3** And White soon won.

9. Shirov-Yuffa
Moscow rapid 2020

39.♖f7 39.♖xh4 gxf3 is far less convincing. **39...♖f8!?** 39...g5 loses to e.g. 40.♖xh4 ♕xh4 41.d5. **40.♖hf3!!** 40.♖xh4 ♖xf7+ 41.♔g1 (41.♔e2 ♕f8!) 41...♖xh4 42.♕xf7 ♕e1+ 43.♔f2 ♕c1+ leads to a draw. **40...exf3 41.♖xe7 ♗xe7 42.♕e6** And Black resigned shortly after.

A Sultan that swings

He never was a big fan, but now that he has seen Sultan Khan's games presented in a historical context, **MATTHEW SADLER** is taking a fresh view. And he looks at new opening books. One of them also took him back to the 1930s, when Botvinnik successfully began experimenting with an early g2-g4.

A few years ago, I developed an obsession for the leading British chess players of the early 20th century. At a time when books are written about so many subjects, it seemed odd that no one had looked at this fascinating period in British chess. I started off with multiple winners of the British Championship and I was lucky with my first two choices: F.D. Yates (1884-1932) and H.E. Atkins (1872-1955). The former was a chess professional, a dour, obdurate defender also capable of powerful attacking play (he beat Alekhine twice); the latter was an exceptionally gifted amateur who – in between extended absences from the game – won the British Championship 9 times in 11 attempts.

I annotated many games of theirs (all available on my blog) and was planning to carry on with some more players, but somewhere I hit a wall. The awful truth is that I couldn't find any games I cared to analyse. I did analyse a few games by Sir George Thomas (1881-1972) –

for example, a fine win against Capablanca during the best tournament of his career, Hastings 1934/35 – but after that my enthusiasm faded. Many of the British players were fascinating characters – Sir George Thomas was a fine athlete, winning the All-England badminton championship 21 times and reaching the Wimbledon tennis single quarterfinals in 1911 – but their chess was not as exciting as their lives! One of the players that disappointed me greatly was Sultan Khan. I played through his games from his British Championship victory in Ramsgate 1929 and couldn't believe what I was seeing. Sultan Khan outlasted his opponents... but they all played so badly!

Historical background

So, when I got *Sultan Khan* by Daniel King (New In Chess) I was greatly intrigued. I had talked to Daniel a year ago and he had hinted that he was working on an exciting but still secret project and I guess this was it!

It's a wonderful book. Having read it, it's clear that the key to understanding Sultan Khan's games and achievements is in context, both on a historical level and on a chess level. King provides a lot of historical background for growing tensions between Great Britain and India in the 1930s through his description of the activities of Umar Hayat Khan, Sultan Khan's employer. It's a subject I knew extremely little about, as colonialism was not broached in history lessons at school, so I learnt something about history in general, too (how often can you say that with a chess book?). Most importantly of all, however, King provides a lot of chess context about Sultan Khan's background and how he learnt chess.

Sultan Khan learnt to play chess according to the Indian rules and only switched to Western chess as an adult (he had probably played Western chess for about three years when he came to England). The Indian rules were not standardized so it is difficult to be sure exactly which form Sultan Khan played, but typical elements were the pawns moving just one square forwards, different promotion rules, no castling and a different setup of the pieces. When you grasp this, you can thoroughly understand how the opening phase of the game could cause Sultan Khan so many difficulties (he was vulnerable to opening disasters throughout his career) and his tendency – especially in his earlier games – to leave his king in the centre. It's also worth noting that he was unable to read any European language, so the entire canon of chess literature was closed to him! I can compare this to the experience I have had learning and playing shogi (Japanese chess) since last year. There's a limited amount of English-language literature available and however hard I try, proper shogi players keep telling me my moves are odd!

Once you understand the reason for the unevenness in Sultan Khan's play, then you can appreciate much better the powerful qualities that allowed him to win the British Championship

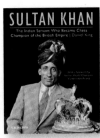

**Sultan Khan
by Daniel King
New In Chess, 2020**
★★★★★

three times and finish highly-placed in international tournaments between 1929 and 1933. For the period he was a good endgame player and tactician, an exceptionally tough defender and he remained capable of unconventional play – sometimes for the worse, but also often for the better. Look at this stunning game (not in the databases), played against the strong English amateur R.P. Michell!

**R.P. Michell
Sultan Khan**
Surrey-Middlesex match 1932
Nimzo-Indian Defence, Spielmann Variation

1.d4 ♘f6 2.c4 e6 3.♘c3 ♗b4
4.♕b3 c5 5.dxc5 ♘c6 6.♘f3 ♘e4
7.♗d2 ♘xd2 8.♘xd2 f5 9.e3 ♗xc5
10.♗e2 0-0 11.0-0 g5 12.♖fd1 g4
13.♘a4 ♗e7 14.♖ac1 b6 15.a3
♗a6 16.♘c3 ♗b7 17.♘b5 ♘e5
18.♘f1 h5 19.♘g3 h4 20.♘h5 h3

'Khan is having fun. It's also very powerful, if followed up correctly. This is true hypermodern chess, advancing the flank pawns to take control of the diagonal. I cannot imagine any English

The key to understanding Sultan Khan's games and achievements is in context, both on a historical level and on a chess level

player of the era playing in the same style.'
21.♘f4 ♕b8 'Instead 21...♖f6 would safeguard the pawn chain and maintain the attack.' **22.c5** 'A powerful move and it should have led to a win after Black's reply.' **22...bxc5**

23.♘xe6 '23.♖xd7 ♘xd7 24.♕xe6+ ♖f7 25.♕g6+ ♗g7 26.♗c4+ is the clearest way to win. Over the next few moves the advantage swings back and forth before Khan settles matters. I am sure that time pressure played a part.'
23...c4 24.♗xc4 dxe6 25.♗xe6+ ♔h8 26.♗d5 ♖c8 27.♖xc8+ ♕xc8 28.e4 ♖b8 29.♕g3 ♘g6 30.♘xa7 ♕f8 31.gxh3 ♗xd5 32.♖xd5 ♖xb2 33.♖xf5 ♕xf5

0-1, in view of 34.exf5 ♖b1+ 35.♔g2 ♘h4+ 36.♕xh4+ ♗xh4.
A book I read with truly great pleasure, and a fantastic addition to chess literature! 5 stars!

■ ■ ■

Botvinnik's sharp push

Now on to *Attacking with g2-g4* by Dmitry Kryakvin (New In Chess). I'm afraid I had to look up the author, as his name was completely unfamiliar to me: he's a 2594-rated Russian GM born in 1984. There are so many strong players in the world nowadays!

I found the idea behind the book extremely appealing: to describe the historical evolution of the sharp g2-g4 push (essentially starting with Botvinnik's games) and then examine a range of openings in which this sharp push has been used. There's a range of the familiar (such as Shirov's famous 7.g4 system against the Semi-Slav) and the zany (such as Murey's 4.g4 in the Grünfeld: 1.d4 ♘f6 2.c4 g6 3.♘c3 d5 4.g4). In a fit of nationalistic chauvinism, I had always thought that this was the English GM Jim Plaskett's idea, but Murey was at it already in 1975! As you can infer from the above, the focus is entirely on 1.d4 / 1.♘f3 openings: no g2-g4 thrusts in Open Sicilians here unfortunately, although there is still plenty of attacking action to see!

The introductory first three chapters are fascinating, tracing the lineage of the g2-g4 thrust through Botvinnik's games and the writings of Isaak Lipnitsky. Every time I go back to Botvinnik's games from the 1930s, I am even more impressed: so many of his concepts make a completely modern impression.

For example, look at this game played against the strong master and well-known theoretician Veniamin Sozin.

**Mikhail Botvinnik
Veniamin Sozin**
Leningrad 1933
Nimzo-Indian Defence, Spielmann Variation

1.d4 ♘f6 2.c4 e6 3.♘c3 ♗b4
4.♕b3 c5 5.dxc5 ♘c6 6.♗g5 h6
7.♗xf6
Part of a process of experimentation that you see in Botvinnik's games around this time. He had tried both 6.♘f3 and then 6.♗g5 h6 7.♗h4 in earlier games. Despite winning in 19

Attacking with g2-g4
by Dmitry Kryakvin
New In Chess, 2019
★★★★☆

moves after 6.♗g5 h6 7.♗h4, he was dissatisfied and tried another idea!
7...♕xf6 8.♘f3 ♗xc5 9.e3 0-0 10.0-0-0 Very aggressive!
10...♕e7 11.♗e2 a6 12.g4

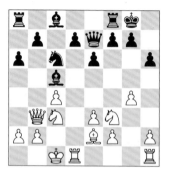

Here it is! This thrust gains additional impetus through the 'hook' on h6 and the tempo Black spends on redeploying the queen to avoid being hit with ♘e4.
12...b5 13.g5 No hesitation!
13...♘a5 14.♕c2 bxc4 15.gxh6 g6 16.♖hg1 ♔h7 17.h4

And the attack continues!
17...♖g8 18.h5 d6 And now, as Botvinnik pointed out in one of his volumes of annotated games, 19.hxg6+ fxg6 20.♖xg6 ♖xg6 21.♖g1 ♕f6 22.♘h4 ♕f5 23.♕xf5 exf5 24.♖xg6, with the threat of

♘d5, would have been the cleanest. Botvinnik played **19.♘g5+ ♔h8 20.♘ce4** and won in 42 moves.

Kryakvin makes the excellent point that the shock effect of Botvinnik's g2-g4 was so great that his opponent's 'first reaction was often wrong. The dreaded pawn almost seems to have hypnotized opponents and stopped them finding the correct reply'.

Having set the scene Kryakvin goes on to examine g2-g4 in a series of 1.d4 openings, and I certainly discovered a few ideas of which I was unaware.

All-in-all I enjoyed this book greatly. I like such examinations of a single theme across history and different openings very much: for me, it's an excellent way of learning and retaining new information easily. It's somewhere between 3 and 4 stars, but I'll give it a special lockdown bonus and bump it up to 4 stars! Recommended!

■ ■ ■

The Modernized Delayed Benoni by Ivan Ivanisevic (Thinkers Publishing) is much more than the title makes you think! When I saw the title, I assumed that the book would be covering a somewhat offbeat system...
1.d4 ♘f6 2.c4 c5 3.d5 g6

... that allows you active play while avoiding too much opening theory. Well, there is some of that in the book's 236 pages, but there is also some heavy Modern Benoni/King's Indian theory in here! In particular, the section on the Sämisch lines 4.♘c3 ♗g7 5.e4 d6 6.f3 e6 and then 7.♘ge2, 7.♗e3 and 7.♗g5 is replete with novelties and attacking ideas. I like the author's approach very much: it is a mixture of a personal journey and a theoretical manual. The author has been probably the main exponent of this line for the past ten years and he uses many of his games to illustrate the variations he has recommended.

The section on the main variation **4.♘c3 ♗g7 5.e4 d6 6.♘f3 0-0 7.h3 e6 8.♗d3** is instructive, as the author 'shows the development of my understanding of this variation as it changed while I played it as Black'.

So, the author explains why he started off with 8...♘a6 and then moved on to 8...♘bd7. He also examines 8...exd5, which Tal once used to conjure up a wonderful attacking display against Vladimirov.

One of the biggest problems I have when taking up a new opening is that I don't have all the emotions – the triumphs, the disasters, the funny things that happened during one game, that I have with my standard repertoire. Playing a new opening can feel cold and unfamiliar. Having a grasp of the history and evolution of a variation really helps me from that point of view: it gives me the feeling that I'm doing more than just repeating moves, I'm continuing logically from the efforts of chess players before me. Although the book is again extremely detailed, there is careful attention to move orders and enough passages of explanation to

Having a grasp of the history of a variation gives me the feeling that I am doing more than just repeating moves

The Modernized Delayed Benoni
by Ivan Ivanisevic
Thinkers Publishing, 2019
★★★★☆

make much of it understandable for non-experts. An excellent effort – 4 stars!

■ ■ ■

You don't have to be called Ivan to write for Thinkers Publishing... but it helps! After Ivan Sokolov and Ivan Ivanisevic, we have a new Ivan – my Guildford teammate Ivan Cheparinov – with Volume 1 of *Cheparinov's 1.d4!*, dealing with the Grünfeld and the King's Indian.

This repertoire book is cutting-edge theory, recommending f3 for White against the fianchetto systems. In fact, at the time of writing this column, Ding and Nepomniachtchi fought out a theoretical line analysed in depth in this book.

**Ding Liren
Ian Nepomniachtchi**
Magnus Carlsen Invitational
chess24.com 2020 (10.2)
Neo-Grünfeld Defence

1.d4 ♘f6 2.c4 g6 3.f3 d5 4.cxd5 ♘xd5 5.e4 ♘b6 6.♘c3 ♗g7 7.♗e3 0-0 8.♕d2 ♘c6 9.0-0-0 ♕d6 10.♘b5 ♕d7 11.♔b1 a6 12.♘c3 ♖d8 13.d5 ♕e8 14.♕c1 ♘a7 15.h4 ♘b5 16.♘ge2 e6 17.h5 exd5 18.hxg6

18...fxg6 18...hxg6 was the line Cheparinov preferred for Black, when his analysis went on in some depth for another 12 moves. 18...fxg6 was one of Cheparinov's sidelines.
19.♗xb6 cxb6 20.♘xd5 ♗e6 21.♘ef4 ♗f7 22.♘xb5 axb5

23.a3 Only here does Ding deviate from Cheparinov's analysis. 23.♕c2 ♖dc8 24.♕b3 ♖c4 25.♘d3 was Cheparinov's line with a slight advantage for White. **23... g5 24.♘c7 ♕e5 25.♘xa8 ♖xa8 26.♘d5 h6 27.♕c3 ♕e6 28.♕b4 ♔h7 29.♖d2 ♖c8 30.♕e7 ♕g6 31.♕xb7 ♖c6 32.♕d7 ♖c5 33.♘e7 ♕f6 34.♘f5** 1-0.

There is a tremendous amount of original ideas and analysis in this book. I was intrigued what Cheparinov recommended against Ivan Ivanisevic's lines in the *The Modernized Delayed Benoni*! As it happens, it's 1-0 to Cheparinov in that regard, as he both considers Ivanisevic's subtle move order in depth, and then suggests a move that Ivanisevic does not consider!
1.d4 ♘f6 2.c4 g6 3.f3 c5 4.d5 ♗g7 5.♘c3 d6 6.e4 e6
Ivanisevic is insistent on playing this before castling, specifically to meet the ♘ge2 system Cheparinov recommends as aggressively as possible.
7.♘ge2 exd5 8.cxd5 ♘bd7
Once the g1-knight has moved to e2, then the black knight on b8 can move to d7. If Black plays ...♘bd7 too early, then White can develop the knight via h3 to f2 which is a safe and harmonious position.

Cheparinov's 1.d4!
by Ivan Cheparinov
Thinkers Publishing, 2019
★★★★☆

9.♘g3 h5 10.♗e2 ♘h7

This clever move avoids the pin on the knight with ♗g5 and stops White from castling.
11.♗e3 Preparing castling by preventing ...♗d4+.
11.0-0 ♗d4+ 12.♔h1 h4 wins a piece.
11...h4 12.♘f1
Black has chased the knight to f1 only once White has developed the bishop to e3, taking away a natural square for the knight on f1! Subtle move orders! Cheparinov's solution is 11.♘f1 before 11.♗e3...

... which as far as I can see is not considered by Ivanisevic! There have just been two games in this line (one of which is Cheparinov's) and it has scored 2/2 so that's not bad for an opening recommendation! Once again, it's definitely a book for experts, but a really good one! 4 shining stars!

■ ■ ■

The advent of superhuman strength engines has revolutionized the quality of chess books and especially opening books. When you read a modern opening book, you can be sure that all the lines have been verified by computers and that the book is devoid of tactical blunders. (That's actually a reason why I'm so partial to books written in the pre-computer age: I find it good training for my tactical alertness to attempt to spot analytical mistakes.) However making use of this 'infallibility' while keeping the book 'human' is the challenge for modern authors.

Kaufman's New Repertoire for Black and White by Larry Kaufman (New In Chess) takes a very unusual approach. Larry Kaufman is a pretty amazing guy: he gained the GM title in 2008, when he won the World Senior Championship, he was one of the strongest Western shogi players and also a strong Chinese chess player, and he's been one of the brains behind the strong Komodo engine. This 400+ page book presents a complete opening repertoire for White and Black, built up from a mixture of human experience (Kaufman's) and explicitly shaped by the lines that two engines – Komodo of course, and Leela Zero – rated highest during extended analysis. Kaufman's goal as White is to find less-analysed but still promising paths in the 1.e4 repertoire (for example, one of the lines he looks at in the Caro-Kann is 1.e4 c6 2.d4 d5 3.♘c3 dxe4 4.♘xe4 ♗f5 5.♕f3), whereas with Black he takes 1.d4 head on with the Grünfeld, whereas against 1.e4 he looks at both the Marshall and the Breyer.

Extremely thorough

It's a book about which my opinion has varied wildly at various times. Firstly, Kaufman does an excellent job of providing multiple options for White and Black within the repertoire he recommends; there's no danger of having to abandon the entire repertoire if one line falls into disrepute. Secondly, the book is clearly and logically organised, and extremely thorough: pretty much all the important lines get covered, which is impressive for such an ambitious book. The difficulty I have with the book is the way the computer analysis is presented. Let me give an example:

1.e4 e6 2.d4 d5 3.♘d2 c5 4.♘gf3 cxd4 5.♘xd4 ♘c6 6.♗b5 ♗d7 7.♘xc6 bxc6 8.♗d3 ♗d6 9.♕e2
And now Kaufman looks at the sideline **9...e5**

The following line is given without comment:
10.exd5 cxd5 11.c4 ♘e7 12.cxd5 ♘xd5 13.♘f3 0-0 14.0-0 ♘f6 15.♘xe5 ♖e8 16.f4 ♘g4 17.♗xh7+ ♔xh7 18.♕d3+ ♔g8 19.♕xd6 ♗b5 20.♕xd8 ♖axd8 21.♖e1 f6 22.h3 ♘xe5 23.fxe5 ♖xe5 24.♗f4

'(+0.37) Black should be able to draw this pawn-down rook and bishops of opposite-colour endgame, but only White can hope to win' – Kaufman.

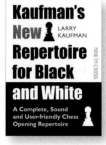

Kaufman's New Repertoire for Black and White by Larry Kaufman New In Chess, 2019 ★★★☆☆

I don't know about you, but during that sequence I was second-guessing almost all of White's and Black's moves! I will certainly not be right, but to play this in a practical game, I would need to work out all the tactics that crop up along the way, but that the engines effortlessly parry in their own silicon brains and don't feel are worth mentioning!

I also wondered about the balance of the analysis: in a positional line, a 20-move computer variation is not so useful (there are so many different options along the way), whereas in a tactical line as above, you'd probably want to see more than one main line.

So, as you can imagine, I was getting somewhat dubious about the whole concept, but I decided – since it's lockdown and there's all the time in the world – to try out some of the openings in blitz and see how they felt. And after a little practice, I felt that Kaufman has chosen his lines well and that this repertoire really would be a good and durable one. So, I'm somewhat torn in my opinion!

I think the average club player could do very well to use the lines Kaufman has distilled as the basis for their repertoire. The club player knows that his main line in each opening is the choice of two strong engines and thus 'tactics-safe' in principle. However, there are some lines/side variations in which a single computer line is given, which are tricky enough to cause confusion if your opponent has the temerity to vary! I think you will need some extra engine checking in a few spots to beef up some of the recommendations enough for practical play. 3 stars! ■

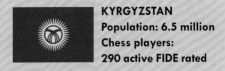

by Han Schut

They are **The Champions**

With nearly all over-the-board chess tournaments cancelled, many of our national champions remain champions for longer than normal. This also goes for NM Alexandra Samaganova, who became women's champion of Kyrgyzstan in April 2019 for the fourth time. After winning her first eight games, which included beating runner up WFM Begimai Zairbek Kyzy in their encounter in Round 4, she secured her championship with a quick draw in the final round.

Both of Alexandra's parents played chess competitively, but her mother, WIM Irina Ostry, undoubtedly had the most significant impact on her chess. Most of the time, this has been a benefit, but as Alexandra explains, sometimes it was a mixed blessing. For example, she competed with her mother at several National Championships (all draws!). They also played in several Chess Olympiads together. Although it is nice to prepare together before the game, it is not easy when your mother is watching your game, especially when you are a time-trouble addict.

Alexandra has already competed in seven Chess Olympiads. One of her highlights was meeting Garry Kasparov in Tromsø in 2014, where he gave her a signed copy of *My Great Predecessors*. In Batumi 2018, she disappointingly lost in Round 9 in a very long game against the United Arab Emirates. To her surprise, she was paired in Round 10 against IM Deimante Cornette, who was rated more than 400 points higher. Before her game, Alexandra decided to go for a long walk to clear her mind and forego preparation. Her strategy paid off: she slowly

ALEXANDRA SAMAGANOVA
Kyrgyzstan

outplayed her opponent, which culminated in Alexandra winning a piece in shared time-trouble.

Alexandra Samaganova (2024)
Deimante Cornette (2462)
Batumi Olympiad 2018

position after 38... ♕g5

Black attacks the pawn on e3, but overlooks her weak back rank. White won a piece and the game with:
39.♖d8+ ♖xd8 40.♕xd8+ ♔h7

41.♕xa8 ♕xe3 42.♔f1 e4 43.♕c8 ♔g6 44.♕c5 ♕c3 45.fxe4 ♘xe4 46.♗h5+ ♔f6 47.♕c6+ ♔g5 48.♕xe4 ♔xh5 49.♕f5+ g5 50.♕xf7+ ♔g4 51.♕e6+ and White won quickly.

With a full-time job as a document-control specialist at the gold mining company Charaat Zaav, Alexandra only has time to play a handful of tournaments each year. She loves to travel for chess, learn about other cultures, and meet other chess players. Fortunately, nowadays, you can connect with chess friends in the virtual world. Alexandra is a social media butterfly and popular on Instagram, Twitter, and chess.com. She started streaming on Twitch nine months ago. Like many gamers, she has created her own Discord server, ♕**Alexandrastan**, a private chat environment for her community. Although her channel is mostly about chess and her Twitch streams, she also discusses food, music, and movies. Alexandra is also teaming up with her followers to train together, like solving puzzles and studying books, including *The Woodpecker Method* (Smith & Tikkanen) and *Grandmaster Preparation: Calculation* (Aagaard). Alexandra has a soft spot for cats and even created a charity for the protection of Kyrgyzstan's big cat, the snow leopard, and has adopted one... virtually. ∎

In **They are The Champions** we pay tribute to national champions across the globe. For suggestions please write to editors@newinchess.com.

Johan-Sebastian Christiansen

CURRENT ELO: 2612

DATE OF BIRTH: June 10, 1998

PLACE OF BIRTH: Tønsberg, Norway

PLACE OF RESIDENCE: Sandefjord, Norway

What is your favourite city?
Doha, Qatar.

What was the last great meal you had?
Pizza, yesterday in my apartment,

What drink brings a smile to your face?
Battery Fresh Energy drink with ice cubes.

Which book would you give to a friend?
The Boy in the Striped Pyjamas by John Boyne.

What book is currently on your bedside table?
The Complete Chess Swindler by David Smerdon.

What is your all-time favourite movie?
Beasts of No Nation.

And your favourite TV series?
Sunderland 'Till I Die.

Do you have a favourite actor?
Sacha Baron Cohen.

And a favourite actress?
Jennifer Aniston.

What music do you listen to?
Electro music.

Is there a work of art that moves you?
No, unless it's a sculpture that falls on me. Then I get moved physically.

Who is your favourite chess player of all time?
Alexander Morozevich, for his wild and attacking games.

Is there a chess book that had a profound influence on you?

The entire 'The English Opening' series by Mihail Marin.

What was your best result ever?
My 2-0 win against Wojtaszek, ranked 19 in the world, in the 2019 World Cup.

What was the most exciting chess game you ever saw?
Nothing beats the games of Jorden van Foreest when he is testing his skills against the world elite. As his second, my heart rate tends to shoot to the sky.

What is your favourite square?
The square you move the pawn to as you enter my beloved English Opening, c4.

Do chess players have typical shortcomings?
I know of someone who can be totally absent during a conversation and say 'Sorry, what did you say again? I was thinking about my game'.

Do you have any superstitions?
I develop rituals during tournaments. Waking up at the same time, going for lunch at the same time, etc. etc...

Facebook, Instagram, Snapchat, or?
Instagram.

How many friends do you have on Facebook?
Let me check. 1575, that's way too many.

Who do you follow on Twitter?
Lots of football teams and players. And friends and chess players.

What is your life motto?
If tomorrow isn't the due date, today isn't the do date.

When were you happiest?
Perhaps on my way to my first Olympiad.

When was the last time you cried?
When our cat sadly passed away.

Which three people would you like to invite for dinner?
Frank Lampard, Sacha Baron Cohen and Ötzi.

What is the best piece of advice you were ever given?
'Don't make the red moves' – Mom.

What would people be surprised to know about you?
That I am lactose intolerant. Jorden always forgets, even though I've told him around 1000 times. So that must surprise many, since it even surprises people who already know!

Where is your favourite place in the world?
I thoroughly enjoyed Florida.

What is your greatest fear?
Oofff... heights... definitely heights...

How do you relax?
Playing FIFA in the living room with something good to drink.

What does it mean to be a chess player?
It means bragging about places you've been to around the world and then completely freezing when the person asks: 'What did you see? What did you do?'

What is the best thing that was ever said about chess?
'Chess is 99% tactics' – Richard Teichmann. I've had 'Chess is 100% tactics' in my chess24 bio without knowing that Teichmann almost said the same.